POWER

DIVINE AND HUMAN

POWER

DIVINE AND HUMAN

*Christian and Muslim
Perspectives*

A Record of the Sixteenth
Building Bridges Seminar

Hosted by Georgetown University
May 8–12, 2017

**LUCINDA MOSHER
DAVID MARSHALL**
EDITORS

Georgetown University Press / Washington, DC

Library of Congress Cataloging-in-Publication Data

Names: Building Bridges Seminar (16th : 2017 : Warrenton, Va.), author. |
    Mosher, Lucinda, editor. | Marshall, David, 1963- editor.
Title: Power : Divine and Human : Christian and Muslim Perspectives : a record
    of the Sixteenth Building Bridges Seminar hosted by Georgetown University,
    May 8/12, 2017 / Lucinda Mosher and David Marshall, editors.
Other titles: Record of the Sixteenth Building Bridges Seminar
Description: Washington, DC : Georgetown University Press, 2019. | Includes
    bibliographical references and index.
Identifiers: LCCN 2019005029 (print) | LCCN 2019022055 (ebook) | ISBN
    9781626167285 (hardcover : qalk. paper) | ISBN 9781626167292 (pbk.
    : qalk. paper) | ISBN 9781626167308 (ebook : qalk. paper)
Subjects: LCSH: Power (Christian theology)—Congresses. | Christianity and
    politics—Congresses. | Islam and politics—Congresses. | Christianity and
    other religions—Islam—Congresses. |
    Islam—Relations—Christianity—Congresses.
Classification: LCC BT738.25 (ebook) | LCC BT738.25 .B85 2017 (print) | DDC
    261.2/7—dc23
LC record available at https://lccn.loc.gov/2019005029

♾ This book is printed on acid-free paper meeting the requirements of the American National Standard for Permanence in Paper for Printed Library Materials.

20 19   9 8 7 6 5 4 3 2   First printing

Printed in the United States of America.

Cover design by Debra Naylor.

Contents

PART FOUR: POLITICAL POWER AND FAITH

PART FIVE: REFLECTIONS

Participants in
Building Bridges Seminar 2017

Hussein Abdulsater, University of Notre Dame, USA

Asma Afsaruddin, Indiana University, USA

Ahmet Alibašić, University of Sarajevo, Bosnia & Herzegovina

Ovamir Anjum, University of Toledo, USA

Mehdi Azaiez, Katholieke Universiteit Leuven, Belgium

Jonathan Chaplin, Tyndale House, Cambridge, UK

Stephen L. Cook, Virginia Theological Seminary, USA

Maria Massi Dakake, George Mason University, USA

Gavin D'Costa, University of Bristol, UK

Susan Eastman, Duke University Divinity School, USA

Brandon Gallaher, University of Exeter, UK

Sidney Griffith, Catholic University of America, USA

Damian Howard, SJ, Heythrop College, University of London, UK

Tuba Işık, University of Paderborn, Germany

Ann Jervis, Wycliffe College, Canada

Azza Karam, United Nations, USA

Jacqueline E. Lapsley, Princeton Theological Seminary, USA

Daniel Madigan SJ, Georgetown University, USA

David Marshall, Georgetown University, USA

Thomas Michel, SJ, Georgetown University, USA

Mahan Mirza, University of Notre Dame, USA

Lucinda Mosher, Hartford Seminary, USA

Martin Nguyen, Fairfield University, USA

Joan O'Donovan, The University of Edinburgh, UK

Elizabeth Phillips, University of Cambridge, UK

Shirin Shafaie, Oxford University, UK

Philip Sheldrake, Westcott House, University of Cambridge, UK

Introduction

Founded in 2002 as an initiative of the Archbishop of Canterbury and under the stewardship of Georgetown University since 2012, the Building Bridges Seminar is an annual international gathering of scholar-practitioners of Islam and Christianity for the purpose of deep dialogical study of texts—scriptural and otherwise—selected to provoke complex discussion of a carefully framed theme, such as revelation, prophethood, prayer, science and religion, or human destiny. Meetings have been held in many locales—among them, Qatar, Bosnia-Herzegovina, Singapore, Rome, and the United Kingdom. The conversation circle is always well balanced, with Christians and Muslims in nearly equal number and women well represented in both cohorts. While most Christian participants have been Anglican or Roman Catholic, care has been taken to include Orthodox and Protestant scholars. Similarly, most Muslim participants have been Sunni, but Shi'a have always taken part. This book presents the proceedings of the sixteenth Building Bridges Seminar, which took place May 8–12, 2017, at the Airlie Center in Warrenton, Virginia. Chaired by Daniel A. Madigan SJ, the Jeanette W. and Otto J. Ruesch Family Associate Professor in Georgetown's Department of Theology, the Seminar's theme was Power—Divine and Human: Christian and Muslim Perspectives.

The Building Bridges Seminar had turned to the theme of power on the heels of robust discussion of monotheism during its 2016 convening. When addressing matters of monotheism and power, the planners found themselves in somewhat parallel situations. On both questions, the received wisdom is that one tradition has basically resolved the issue and the other has not: "everyone knows" that Christians have difficulty substantiating their claim to be monotheists, just as "everyone knows" that Muslims have difficulty distinguishing between God's power and their own. Any dialogical framework for examining either theme would ask hard questions of the scriptures and authoritative traditions of both religions. The Building Bridges Seminar's method of studying together provides a framework within which adherents of each religion demonstrate for the other how they have grappled with and are in fact still grappling with those questions. And in watching each other wrestle with the larger issue from within the particularities of our respective traditions, we gain insights into the complexity of what we might have thought were settled questions for our own tradition.

Setting the tone for the 2017 seminar was a preliminary session on the evening of May 8. Held in Georgetown University's Riggs Library and open to the public, the session featured a pair of introductory lectures: "The Power of God and Islam's Regime of Power on Earth," by Jonathan Brown (Georgetown University); and "Religion and Power: A Christian Perspective," by Philip Sheldrake (Wescott House, Cambridge). These papers, offered in part 1 of this volume, provide an overview of issues involved in discussions of divine power, the human exercise of power, and whatever interrelationship there may be between the two.

Seminar participants were then transported to the Airlie Center in Warrenton, Virginia, for four full days of closed meetings in a retreat-like setting. As has long been the Seminar's custom, the daily schedule provided for a morning plenary session during which a scholar delivered an exegetical paper introducing the texts designated for the day's close reading and deep discussion. For the remaining minutes, plenary discussion would ensue. Participants would then transition to study in one of four predetermined groups that remained constant throughout the seminar for two 2.5 hour sessions of intense discussion of the day's material. An hour-long pre-dinner plenary offered an opportunity for each small group to share its insights with the others. Communal meals encouraged further consideration of ideas that had emerged.

In 2017, days 1 and 2 of dialogical text-study focused on the question of God's power and authority. What kind of power is it? What has God revealed of it? Where do we believe humanity has witnessed God's power demonstrated in a defining way? What do we make of the paradoxes of divine power—justice and mercy, judgment and forgiveness, liberation and constraint, absoluteness and closeness, insistence and patience, wrath and love, to name but a few? In order to make sure that we explored both traditions in their particularity rather than just superficially conflating them, the whole of day 1 was devoted to the Qur'an and hadith, and the whole of day 2 to biblical texts. These texts are provided in part 2 of this volume, along with brief essays introducing them: "The Contours of God's Power: An Introduction to Passages from the Qur'an and Hadith" by Martin Nguyen (Fairfield University) and "Biblical Conceptions of Power—Divine and Human" by Stephen Cook (Virginia Theological Seminary).

For day 3, the focus was on the nature of a human life and a human community that has recognized God's power (in the diverse ways it is understood) and has accepted to be subject to it. It was noted that, in both traditions, the image of the servant—even the slave—is key to understanding the nature of the believer. And in both, the community of believers is considered to have a divinely willed existence: it is to be iconic for humanity. What does a human community truly subject to God's power look like? These matters were treated in two half-day sessions—one devoted to each tradition. A range of textual material was considered: more Qur'an and Hadith but also items such as an excerpt from the writings of Ayatullah Ruhullah Khumayni on Islamic government; more Bible passages but also items such as a portion of Saint Augustine's *City of God*. See part 3 of these proceedings for day 3's foundational essays: "Ideals and Realities of Muslim Community Ordering" by Ahmet Alibašić (University of Sarajevo) and "From Nation to Church: The Community of God's Rule" by Joan O'Donovan (The University of Edinburgh)—plus the texts these papers introduce.

On day 4, as on day 3, the seminar's conversations were not about ideals alone; they were also realistic considerations of our continual failures to embody those ideals and of the way ideals are so easily co-opted and subverted by all-too-human forms of power. Again divided in half, thus devoting equal time to each tradition, day 4 examined the role of the community of believers in the broader world. Can the community exercise power? Is it obliged to do so? (Indeed, there are politically quietist strains in both traditions.) If so, what kind of power? In its search for possible responses, the seminar was determined to look at texts of each tradition that answer these questions in ways that some might find problematic but that have shaped and sometimes continue to shape attitudes and policy. What kind of politics and economics correspond to the understandings we have of God's power? What place is there for force, resistance, compulsion, violence, and nonviolence? In part 4 we offer the day 4 lectures on political power and faith: an Islamic perspective in "The Role of the Community in the Broader World" by Mahan Mirza (University of Notre Dame) and "Faith and Political Power: A 'Non-Establishment' Reading of the Christian Tradition" by Jonathan Chaplin (Tyndale House, Cambridge). In part 4 is also found the texts studied on day 4. The Christian collection includes yet more Bible passages plus examples of the thinking of John of Salisbury, John Calvin, and Pope Paul VI; in the Islamic collection, yet more Qur'an and hadith but also the Marrakesh Declaration (January 2016).

In short, the task of the authors of the essays found in parts 2, 3, and 4 of this volume was to introduce a set of texts that had been chosen for their potential for sparking a deep conversation around a particular theological theme. Our purpose in providing these exegetical essays and collections of texts for study organized as we ourselves took them up is to encourage our readers to dig into the texts—be that as individuals, as students in a university course, or as members of an ongoing dialogue, which, as its name implies, requires time, patience, and ongoing commitment.

The hallmark of the Building Bridges Seminar is the opportunity for Christians and Muslims to watch each other grapple with questions important to us and between us—and to offer theological hospitality to each other as we do so. To offer our readers a glimpse into this process, part 5 provides a digest of reflections on the Building Bridges Seminar process and the content of its sixteenth convening, provided by four scholars for whom 2017 was their first experience of the project.

Readers who wish to undertake further exploration of topics central to this book might consider Talal Asad, *Genealogies of Religion: Disciplines and Reasons of Power in Christianity and Islam in Christianity and Islam* (Baltimore: Johns Hopkins University Press, 1993); or John J. Donohue, SJ, and Christian W. Troll, SJ, eds., *Faith, Power, and Violence: Muslims and Christians in a Plural Society, Past and Present* (Rome: Pontificio Istituto Orientale, 1998); or Paul Heck, *Common Ground: Islam, Christianity, and Religious Pluralism* (Washington, DC: Georgetown University Press, 2009); or John Renard's *Islam and Christianity: Theological Themes in Comparative Perspective* (Berkeley: University of California Press, 2011).

In the main text of this volume, diacritics have been kept to a minimum. Dates are "CE" unless otherwise noted.

We are grateful to many publishers for permission to use the material excerpted in this volume. All are credited in course. Unless otherwise noted, Qur'an quotations are according to Seyyed Hossein Nasr, et al., eds., *The Study Quran: A New Translation and Commentary* (New York: HarperOne, 2015)[1] or from Mohammed Marmaduke Pickthall, *The Meaning of the Glorious Qur'ān* (London: Knopf, 1930), modified slightly. Unless otherwise noted, Bible passages are from the Revised Standard Version of the Bible, copyright 1952 by the Division of Christian Education of the National Council of the Churches of Christ in the USA (used by permission; all rights reserved), or the New Revised Standard Version of the Bible, copyright 1989 by the Division of Christian Education of the National Council of the Churches of Christ in the USA (used by permission; all rights reserved). Deep appreciation is extended to Georgetown University president John J. DeGioia for his ongoing support of the Building Bridges Seminar. As in previous years, David Marshall (the project's academic director) and Daniel Madigan (its chair) were instrumental in setting the 2017 theme, organizing the roster of scholars, and—in careful conversation with those designated as presenters—choosing the texts to be studied. Others playing strategic roles in the success of the 2017 gathering included Lucinda Mosher (Hartford Seminary), the Seminar's assistant academic director; Samuel Wagner, who, as coordinator for Catholic and Jesuit Initiatives in the Office of the President, provided logistical support; and Georgetown University's Berkley Center—which also provides an ongoing base of operations and online presence for the Seminar and has made the publication of this book possible. Finally, gratitude is extended to Alfred

Bertrand and the staff of Georgetown University Press for their patient assistance with this project.

Note

1. 105 verses from *The Study Quran: A New Translation and Commentary* by Seyyed Hossein Nasr and Caner K. Dagli. Copyright © 2015 by Seyyed Hossein Nasr. Reprinted by permission of HarperCollins Publishers.

PART ONE

Overviews

The Power of God and Islam's Regime of Power on Earth

JONATHAN BROWN

I remember as a teenager watching the movie *Warlock* (1991) on late-night cable television. *Warlock* is a terrible movie, but I do recall one thing about the plot. A warlock is trying to piece together some ancient parchments that reveal the "true name of God," which the warlock can then use to undo all of creation. I remember the climactic scene, in which the warlock learns the name and screams up to the heavens "Yea, I know Thee!" while clouds whirl and thunder claps loudly like someone trying to stop a college friend from telling an embarrassing story over dinner.

This movie is bad, but it's not unusual. If Hollywood films are any indication, God would seem to have a good number of vulnerabilities, which are routinely poked at by devious fallen angels out to undo His will.[1] In such films, God, the Creator and Sustainer of the universe, is often portrayed much like good King Richard in the Robin Hood tales: out of town and about to be undermined.

And here Hollywood is not entirely innovative. Some (I emphasize *some*) Talmudic writings speak of God as if He is in need of human aid to achieve His will. One midrash tells of God promising to destroy the children of Israel after the episode of the golden calf but then regretting His vow. Moses tells God that he can help Him out of this predicament by means of a legal ruse. Since a rabbi can grant a petitioner a release from a promise, Moses "wrapped himself in his cloak and seated himself like a Sage, and the holy one, blessed be he, stood before him like one petitioning [for the annulment of] his vow."[2] And, of course, in the Hellenic tradition there is Diomedes's glorying in battle before Troy, raging unchecked until he even spears Ares, the god of war himself, in the bowels and sends him howling back to Olympus.[3] David Hume quotes Dione from the poem, "Many ills . . . have the gods inflicted on men; and many ills, in return, have men inflicted on the gods."[4]

I mention this sampler of classics and trash to make the point that a deity need not be all-powerful, invincible, or invulnerable. We see that—in the ancient and modern heritage of the Abrahamic tradition, which French Orientalists imagined as having sprung from a desert world in which God's unity and omnipotence were as clear as the enveloping sky over the barren horizon—God is not necessarily in control.[5] God the Father, God the Creator, can be portrayed as vulnerable to attack, machinations, and manipulation.

But in the Qur'an, the unmistakable desert horizon comes back into view. The theme of God's power and its ramifications is, without a doubt, central to the holy book and is salient in the Islamic theological tradition. One wonders if the Qur'an, which criticizes Jews for allegedly saying, "God's hands are shackled" (Q. 5:64)[6] and vehemently rejects the notion that God could suffer as a human being, sees itself in a large part as a corrective. It brings God's power back into center view (here I am thinking of power as capacity [*qadar*], especially to exert one's will, and power as authority [*sultan*, essentially imperium]). And, historically, it gave birth to a worldview in which power was a main idiom of formatting society and framing relations.

In the Qur'an, God's power is the superlative of all superlatives. It is total, absolute, and without exception. "To Him belongs all that is in the heavens and in the earth; surely God, He is the All-sufficient, the All-laudable" (Q. 22:64); "To God belong the hosts of the heavens and the earth; God is All-mighty, All-wise" (Q. 48:7); and "Whosoever desires glory, the glory altogether belongs to God" (Q. 35:10). "He is God; there is no god but He. He is the King, the All-holy, the All-peaceable, the All-faithful, the All-preserver, the All-mighty, the All-compeller, the All-sublime. Glory be to God, above that they associate! He is God, the Creator, the Maker, the Shaper. To Him belong the Names Most Beautiful. All that is in the heavens and the earth magnifies Him; He is the All-mighty, the All-wise" (Q. 59:23–24). Perhaps the most commonly recited verse of the entire Qur'an is

> God: there is no god but He, the Living, the Everlasting. Slumber seizes Him not, neither sleep; to Him belongs all that is in the heavens and the earth. Who is there that shall intercede with Him save by His leave? He knows what lies before them and what is after them, and they comprehend not anything of His knowledge save such as He wills. His Throne comprises the heavens and earth; the preserving of them oppresses Him not; He is the All-high, the All-glorious. (Q. 2:255)[7]

I could go on and on.

I will go on since the Qur'an seems to do so quite on purpose. God is "never wearied by creation" (Q. 46:33); "He forgives and punishes whomever He wills" (Q. 2:284); everything prostrates to Him, willingly or unwillingly (Q. 13:15; 17:44). In the Qur'an, the metaphors and parables of God's power are awesome:

oceans of ink and forests of pens could not exhaust His words (Q. 18:109; 31:27); if the Qur'an were sent down on a mountain, the very rock would be "shattered asunder out of the fear of God" (Q. 59:21). Nothing man can do could hurt God (Q. 3:144, 176–77; 47:32). Even when God lays down what appear to be theological red lines for Himself, His own power and will yield exceptions. No one can intercede with God, for example, "unless He wills it."

There is no negotiating with God. Abraham's long pleading and bargaining with God over the fate of Sodom (Gen. 18:16–33) is crushed into two lines in the Qur'an. Abraham voices his concern over the impending destruction of righteous folk in the town only once. "O Abraham, turn away from this," the angelic messengers reply curtly. "Truly the command of thy Lord has come, and surely a punishment that cannot be repelled comes upon them" (Q. 11:74). Abraham's worry for the fate of Lot and other pious folk merits a similarly sharp response in another telling of the episode in the Qur'an: "We know better who is in [the city]" (Q. 29:32). Even a common act of desperate bargaining that many Muslim scholars allow—namely, the "O God, if you do [insert request here] for me, I promise I'll [insert promise here]" (in Arabic, this is termed *nadhr al-mujāza*)—is an illusion. The Prophet informs us, "Indeed a vow, it does not hasten or ward off anything. Rather, vows just prevent one from being stingy."[8] No one can actually alter what God has decreed. One cannot *buy* God's will with the promise of some act.[9]

In the Hadith tradition, there is a sort of negotiation that occurs over the number of daily prayers. During Muhammad's miraculous night journey to Jerusalem and ascension through the heavens, it is originally an obligation for *fifty* daily prayers that is revealed to him. On his way down, however, Muhammad meets Moses, who advises him to go back and ask God for less. Muhammad does so four times, eventually ending up with *five* daily prayers. But even this negotiation seems more like a stylized performance. In this report, when Moses suggests to the Prophet that he return a final time and ask for even fewer prayers, "it was called out (presumably in some sonorous voice), 'I have declared what is obligatory and have lightened the burden of My slaves, and I will reward every good deed tenfold.'"[10] It is no more real than a negotiation with a boss who has listened in on your every private word.

Of course, one cannot speak of God's power without some acknowledgment of the problem of theodicy. This question has been debated by Muslim theologians but has not generated the volume of scholarly and popular reflection that has been seen, especially in the last century, within both the Western Christian tradition and Judaism.[11] In my travels in the Muslim world, I have never come across an equivalent of *When Bad Things Happen to Good People* by Rabbi Harold Kushner, a book that has been called "the #1 bestselling inspirational classic from the nationally known spiritual leader; a source of solace and hope for over four-million readers" and has been translated into fifteen languages.[12]

In the late eighth century two schools of thought in the debates over theodicy emerged. The first, upheld by the rationalist Mu'tazila school, affirmed that God was constrained by justice and was unable to do evil (*sharr*). Everything He did thus had to be for the best (*al-aṣlaḥ*, Leibniz-like[13]) since He was incapable of doing or commanding evil. Yet this school of thought was and remains a decidedly minority one. It is as if, in Islam, God's overwhelming power simply swamped anxieties over divine justice. The opposing school, that of the Sunni majority, could be called the Divine Command/Nominalist or even the "Job 38" approach:[14] God is not constrained by justice, God *is* justice. To even ask about why bad things happen to good people is to miss the point. As the Qur'an declares, "He is not asked about what He does. They are asked" (Q. 21:23).

Beyond citing the above Qur'anic verse, the prominent nineteenth-century Muslim theologian Burhan al-Din al-Bajuri (d. 1860) saw it as sufficient to quote a poem by a scholar in the thirteenth century, which he dreamed after hearing of the destruction of Baghdad by the pagan Mongols in 1258:

> Leave aside any objection, for the command is not yours,
> Nor is ordaining the movements of the planets.
> So, do not ask God about what He does,
> Whoever wades into the depths of the ocean will perish.[15]

Now, it is not that Sunnis did not understand the rationalists' concerns over issues like theodicy. Rather, they thought that trying to quiet these concerns through speculative argument was misguided. As one Sunni scholar wrote of the rationalists, "They wanted to describe God by His justice, but in so doing they deprived Him of his due virtue (*fa-akhrajuhu min faḍlihi*)"; the virtue of His power.[16] Sunni theologians over the centuries saw one of their tasks as protecting (ironically) God's power from heretics. For example, according to Sunni theology, God is not even required to reward good deeds and punish bad, despite His numerous statements in the Qur'an about doing so.[17] Although the Qur'an repeats that "God does not break promises" (see Q. 3:9; 13:31; and elsewhere), Sunni theologians have asserted that is it not rationally possible that God could be constrained from doing so if He wanted. It is only God's choice not to break His promises. Of course, Sunni theologians added that, from our mortal perspective pondering God's law (*shar*), it is effectively impossible (*mustaḥīl*) for Him.[18]

This deference to God's power often required impressive grammatical gymnastics, for example, in the argument that fulfilling the promises and threats God had made is "obligatory for God" but not "obligatory upon Him." Ultimately, God is all-powerful, and that means our mortal reason must remain apart from Him and unable to reach Him. We must trust, as the Qur'an declares, that "God does not wrong any of the slaves" (i.e., the slaves of God, in other words, human beings).

The power of God, a power that we ponder as His slaves and as slaves to the medium of created human language, raises the question of how the Qur'an envisions and possibly formats earthly power. That the Qur'an refers over and over to human beings as "the slaves" or the "slaves of God" suggests two possibilities.

On the one hand, the absolute and unquestionable power of God and the utter helplessness of His slaves on earth could yield a framework for radical egalitarianism. Just as the French Orientalists imagined, the desert would shape a people of equals; any inkling of claimed inherent superiority between individuals would be dwarfed into nothingness by the immense vault of the sky and the omnipotent God who had raised it up. Indeed, this vision of how power plays out on earth did come about in Islamic history, although in a minority strain among the early Muslims. The Kharijites were radical egalitarians, following closely the Qur'anic decree that "Indeed the best of you in God's eyes is the most pious" (Q. 49:13). They held that only the most pious Muslim was qualified to lead, and that committing any grave sin was a sign of unbelief. But this led to the autoimmune problem that afflicts many extremist movements: radical, compound meritocracy means that disputes over who truly merits the most, combined with fracturing over the perceived shortcomings of leaders, soon impedes the stability that both state and society need to achieve peace and prosperity. States and societies are inherently hierarchical, and power cannot be dispersed uniformly to and then contested willy-nilly by each individual.

This reality presages the second possibility for how Islamic civilization would understand power in this world. Here the master/slave relationship between God and humanity is reflected in a structure of ordered subordination among humankind. As in some of the writings of the church fathers, the structure of authority in this world mirrors the vertical structure between the heavens and the earth.[19]

The word *'abd* (slave) and its feminine, *ama*, derive from old Semitic roots that appear in the relational pair of subordinate/subject/slave and lord/master (*rabb*). In the Qur'an this becomes the main idiom for the relation between God and humankind. But it is projected into the Qur'anic vision of society as well, repeating itself like floored nested dolls within the ranks of humanity. The Qur'an orders Muslims to "obey God and obey the messenger and those in authority amongst you" (Q. 4:59). And then the Prophet expands this in his teachings:

> Indeed, each of you is a shepherd, and each of you is responsible for his flock. So the ruler [*imam*] in charge of the people is a shepherd, and he is responsible for his flock. And a husband is the shepherd for the people of his household, and he is responsible for them. And a wife is the shepherd of the people of her husband's household and his children, and she is responsible for them. And a man's slave is the shepherd of his master's property, and he is responsible for it.[20]

In fact, as I discovered on a desert outing with Bedouin friends (the French Orientalists would have been envious), the Prophet instructed that, if even three people go out on travel, one of them needs to be placed in charge.[21]

The idiom of slave and lord, however, raises a serious question about the implications of this structure of power. Although the Qur'an repeatedly urges

Muslims to free their slaves and even commands manumission as expiation for certain sins, the holy book takes the existence of the slave/master relationship for granted; it is a structural feature in the world. I remember well reading the following verse for the first time almost twenty years ago: "God sets forth this parable: [on the one hand, we have] a slave controlled by his master, with no power over anything; and [on the other hand, we have] another man We have supplied with good provision from which he gives alms privately and openly. Can they be considered equal?" (Q. 16:75).[22] The Qur'an follows this immediately with a second parable of a person who is mute and unable to accomplish tasks and another who is able. These were hard for me to read. They seemed like judgments that equated conditions beyond a person's control with their existential or moral worth.

But these are not judgments. For the Qur'an, these are statements of relational and economic fact. Relationships of power, of subordination, are natural and human and social. (Think of Confucius's Five Great Relationships, all of which involve an element of subordination. Even the friend-friend relationship is conceived of as between a senior and junior friend.) When Muslim scholars speculated on the theological etiology of slavery as a condition, they settled on it being a punishment for disbelief (since the only people Muslims could enslave were non-Muslims from outside of the Abode of Islam). But this was not passing moral or metaphysical judgment. According to Muslim theologians, those same people, from lands beyond where any reliable knowledge of Islam had spread, were not going to be held accountable for their unbelief on the Day of Judgment. They had done nothing wrong. God would pass judgment on them on other terms.[23] But they dwelled in a pagan sea, and that was structurally below the Abode of Islam.

That slavery was an incidental—if very impactful—status and not a judgment of worth is clear in the fact that a Muslim slave's place in the structure of Muslim society could change dramatically based on other talents he or she possessed. For example, a slave's piety, moral standing, or some other expertise could even result in them being placed in a position of authority above free folk, as the Prophet mentioned when he ordered the Muslims to "heed and obey" their commanders, "even if the one put in charge of you is an Ethiopian slave whose head is [dark] as a raisin."[24]

I would suggest that, in the Islamic worldview, there is a hierarchy of power that was not moral or metaphysical but essentially functional. Thus, men and women are equal before God. They are both created from a single soul (Q. 4:1). Yet, as the Qur'an says, "men have a degree above [women]" (Q. 2:228). But this degree is functional. "Men are responsible over women," the Qur'an states, "by virtue of that which God has favored some over others, and by virtue of their spending of their wealth [in maintenance of them]" (Q. 4:34). So God has "favored" men over women not in any moral or absolute sense but because He created two different genders with complementary capacities. Interestingly,

Muslim jurists generally held that, if a Muslim man could not provide for his womenfolk, his responsibility (and authority) over them lapsed.[25]

So this hierarchy of power did indeed form a world order that was not egalitarian. But this was only because life is not egalitarian. It is not egalitarian because people have different abilities and talents and because they must fulfill different functions. It is not egalitarian because societies need order (hence the desert outing commander). Certainly, the Qur'an and the Prophet strive to break down hierarchies that have no functional basis, such as racial ones. The Prophet declared in his farewell sermon that "the Arab is not superior to the non-Arab, nor the non-Arab to the Arab, nor a red skinned person to a black skinned person, nor a black skinned to a red, except in fear of God."[26] And he totally repudiated tribal chauvinism.

And, finally, life is not egalitarian because, at least outside the liberal tradition, not all aims or objectives are equal. From the Islamic perspective, humans have been told repeatedly by countless prophets what they must do to attain felicity in this life and the next: worship the one God and do good deeds. This certainty about the good in turn results in a power hierarchy among religious traditions. From the Islamic perspective, people who learn about Islam but nonetheless choose not to embrace it have gone astoundingly astray. Now, fascinatingly, the Qur'an and the Prophet's precedent make clear that these religious groups can continue to follow their own religions under Muslim rule, and their rights to do so will be protected. But they are not equal to Muslims. As the Prophet supposedly said in a (not very reliable) hadith, "Islam is exalted. It is not exalted over."[27] For Muslim jurists, this provided evidence that non-Muslims could not inherit from Muslims and that non-Muslims could not build houses taller than those of Muslim neighbors.[28]

I will end with a final point about what I argue is Islam's functional hierarchy of power in the world, and I will end as I began: with late-night cable. I remember, also in high school, watching the exhausting South African miniseries *Shaka Zulu* (1986). At one point in the series the Zulu king is told by British envoys, "A man with Christ in his heart is more powerful than all the armies in the world." Of course, the Zulu king immediately puts these Christians in the front line of his army and tells them to defeat the vast host arrayed against them.

What has always struck me as interesting is that, in all but the grand scale Muslim tellings of history, the locus and deposit of temporal power seem to have little moral or theological dimension. The "wheel of fortune" is theistic, directed by the hand of God, but within the internal sub-cycles of human history that wheel seems not to be spinning some moral teleology of power. I remember sitting in a Friday prayer sermon in Egypt in 2000, and the preacher casually mentioned how a number of the leading Companions of the Prophet had all died in a plague one year. "How can he just say that?" I thought. "These were pillars of Islam, the Prophet's own lieutenants. And they just die in a plague, and no one thinks that's a problem!?"

But Islamic history is absolutely full of this. Pious heroes standing up for justice, beheaded unceremoniously by a despot and their heads stuck on pikes. The Qur'an speaks of prophets being killed. Countless righteous rebellions failed, charismatic scholar-generals were killed by stray bullets.[29] Since the allocation of worldly power has little theological dimension, success or failure has no necessary link to the morality or righteousness of a cause. Victory, defeat, death, and suffering, they are all equally trials from God, "that We may test you," says the Qur'an. "Such days," God says, "We deal out in turn among men, that God may know who are the believers, and that He may take witnesses (martyrs) from among you" (Q. 3:140). It is God "who created death and life so that He might test you [to show] which of you is best in deeds" (Q. 67:2).

The great historian Marshall Hodgson, a Quaker, described Christianity as "a demand for personal responsiveness to redemptive love in a corrupted world." Islam, by contrast, is "a demand for personal responsibility for the moral ordering of the natural world."[30] If the world is fundamentally broken, that brokenness is revealed most traumatically in—from an uninitiated perspective—the ultimate malfunction of power in the world: the execution of the Messiah. In that case, how and when power is allocated and used in this world becomes theologically fraught. But if the world is ordered as God intended it, and it is the duty of human beings only to orient themselves toward God as the natural world does, then the allocation of power within the world is free of such drama. The only question is whether Muslims, who are all slaves of God, should accept among themselves the intrahuman hierarchies of power that are as necessary for peace and prosperity as they are vulnerable to abuse and the dishonor of God's will.

Notes

1. Examples include *The Devil's Advocate* (1997), *Fallen* (1998), and *Dogma* (1999).
2. Christine Hayes, *What's Divine about Divine Law?* (Princeton, NJ: Princeton University Press, 2015), 193.
3. Homer, *Iliad*, 5.900ff.
4. David Hume, *The Natural History of Religion*, in *The Philosophical Works of David Hume* (Edinburgh: Adam Black & Co., 1826), 4:452.
5. See, for example, Ernest Renan's (d. 1892) *De la part des peuples sémitiques dans l'histoire de la civilisation*, and Fromentin's longing "to see a blue sky without clouds above a desert free of shadows" (*de voir le ciel bleu sans nuages et au-dessus le désert sans ombre*); Eugène Fromentin, *Une année dans le Sahel, un été dans la Sahara*, 7th ed. (Paris: Nelson Éditeurs, 1963), 272.
6. In this essay, unless otherwise noted, quotations of the Qur'an are according to the author's own translation.
7. A. J. Arberry, *The Koran Interpreted: A Translation* (New York: George Allen & Unwin, 1955), 65.

8. *Ṣaḥīḥ al-Bukhārī: kitāb al-aymān wa'l-nudhūr, bāb al-wafā' bi'l-nadhr*. Unless otherwise noted, all translations from Arabic sources are the author's.

9. Ibn Ḥajar al-ʿAsqalānī, *Fatḥ al-bārī sharḥ Ṣaḥīḥ al-Bukhārī*, ed. ʿAbd al-ʿAzīz Bin Bāz and Muḥammad Fuʾād ʿAbd al-Bāqī (Beirut: Dār al-Kutub al-ʿIlmiyya, 1997), 11:7–9.

10. *Ṣaḥīḥ al-Bukhārī: kitāb badʾ al-khalq, bāb dhikr al-malāʾika.*

11. It is important to note that this is a largely modern phenomenon. Premodern Christians' attention to the "problem of evil" was far below the scale with which this topic has been addressed by Christian theologians since the middle of the twentieth century. Reflection on the Holocaust has much to do with this, as has general secular questioning of Christianity from the eighteenth century forward.

12. Harold S. Kushner, *When Bad Things Happen to Good People* (New York: Schocken, 1981). Kushner's book is thus described in promotional materials for the 2004 edition from Anchor Books.

13. That is, following Gottfried Wilhelm Leibniz (1646–1716), the philosopher credited with originating the term "theodicy" (literally, "God's justice"). See Eric Ormsby, *Theodicy in Islamic Thought* (Princeton, NJ: Princeton University Press, 1984).

14. In the Bible's book of Job, chapter 38 presents God's response "out of a whirlwind" to Job's lament over the day of his birth (which he voiced in chapter 3).

15. Burhān al-Dīn Ibrāhīm al-Bayjūrī, *Ḥāshiyat al-Imām al-Bayjūrī ʿalā jawharat al-tawḥīd*, ed. ʿAlī Jumʿa (Cairo: Dār al-Salām, 2006), 168, 180–82.

16. This scholar was Shihāb b. Khirāsh. See Shams al-Dīn al-Dhahabī, *Mīzān al-Iʿtidāl*, ed. ʿAlī Muḥammad al-Bijāwī (Cairo: ʿĪsā al-Bābī al-Ḥalabī, 1963–64; repr., Beirut: Dār al-Maʿrifa, n.d.), 2:281.

17. Al-Bayjūrī, *Ḥāshiyat al-Imām al-Bayjūrī*, 180.

18. Al-Bayjūrī, 180–81; Abū Ḥafs ʿUmar al-Māturīdī al-Nasafī et al., *Majmūʿat al-ḥawāshī al-bahiyya ʿalā sharḥ al-ʿaqāʾid al-nasafiyya* (Cairo: Dār al-Muṣṭafā, 2007), 1:147–49.

19. See the "Letters of Ignatius, Bishop of Antioch (d. circa 110 CE)," in Cyril Richardson, ed., *Early Christian Fathers* (New York: Macmillan, 1970), 76.

20. *Ṣaḥīḥ al-Bukhārī: kitāb al-aḥkām, bāb qawluhu taʿālā aṭīʿū Allāh wa aṭīʿū al-rasūl wa ūlī al-amr minkum.*

21. *Sunan* of Abū Dāwūd: *kitāb al-jihād, bāb fī al-qawm yusāfirūn yuʾmarūn aḥaduhum.*

22. Following M. A. S. Abdel Haleem, *The Qurʾan: English Translation* (New York: Oxford University Press, 2010), modified slightly.

23. See Abū al-Ḥasan al-Ashʿarī, *al-Ibāna ʿan uṣūl al-diyāna*, ed. Fawqiyya Ḥusayn Maḥmūd (Cairo: Dār al-Anṣār, 1977), 33.

24. *Ṣaḥīḥ al-Bukhārī: kitāb al-aḥkām, bāb al-samʿ wa'l-ṭāʿa li'l-imām mā lam takun maʿṣiya.*

25. Muḥammad b. Aḥmad al-Qurṭubī, *al-Jāmiʿ li-aḥkām al-qurʾān*, ed. Muḥammad Ibrāhīm al-Ḥifnāwī and Maḥmūd Ḥāmid ʿUthmān, vol. 10 (Cairo: Dār al-Ḥadīth, 1994).

26. Aḥmad Ibn Ḥanbal, *Musnad* (Maymaniyya printing), 5:411.

27. Abū Bakr al-Bayhaqī, *al-Sunan al-kubrā*, ed. Muḥammad ʿAbd al-Qādir ʿAṭā (Beirut: Dār al-Kutub al-ʿIlmiyya, 1999), 6:338; and ʿAbd Raʾūf al-Munāwī, *Fayḍ al-qadīr sharḥ al-jāmiʿ al-ṣaghir*, ed. Ḥamdī al-Damardāsh Muḥammad (Mecca: Maktabat Nizār Muṣṭafā al-Bāz, 1998), 5:2547.

28. Manṣūr al-Buhūtī, *al-Rawḍ al-murbi'*, ed. Bashīr Muḥammad 'Uyūn (Damascus: Maktabat Dār al-Bayān, 1999), 226; Abū Isḥāq al-Shīrāzī, *al-Muhadhdhab* (Beirut: Dār al-Fikr, n.d.), 2:254; and Muḥammad b. Aḥmad al-Sarakhsī, *al-Mabsūṭ* (Beirut: Dār al-Ma'rifa, 1978), 16:134.

29. One such example is Ibn Abī Maḥallī, who died in 1613, in early modern Morocco.

30. Marshall Hodgson, *The Venture of Islam* (Chicago: University of Chicago Press, 1974), 1:337.

Religion and Power

A Christian Perspective

PHILIP SHELDRAKE

This essay introduces, from a Christian standpoint, the theme of religion and power in relation to God's power, the human exercise of power, and how these two interrelate—or fail to interrelate. At the start, I want to highlight two things. First, what follows is only one person's perspective. There is so much material on power in the Bible that I have inevitably had to make choices. However, I hope that what follows is balanced and helpful. Second, my reflections focus mainly on biblical texts. However, in my conclusion I will refer briefly to one contemporary postscriptural resource: the liberation theology of Latin American theologian Gustavo Gutiérrez. He uses biblical texts to focus on God's desire to re-empower the powerless—that is, the materially poor and socially marginalized.

The Meaning of Power

To begin with, what do we mean by power? In English the word has a range of definitions. Overall, it implies the ability to do something. In the public realm it stands for authority, control, or political and social influence. "Power" may also refer to particular prerogatives, such as "the power of the president." We refer to countries with military strength, such as the United States, as "world powers." The word also has a place in mathematical multiplication ("to the power of ten") and in the energy world. We use the word metaphorically, for example, "the powers that be" or "the power behind the throne." Interestingly, in medieval Western Christian imagery, the heavenly angels are organized into a ninefold hierarchy. The sixth level is referred to as "the powers" who maintain the order of the cosmos. Finally, the concept of power also echoes the ambiguous relationship between two Latin words, *potestas* (translated literally as "power") and *potentia*.

While *potentia* also has connotations of power (for example, the word "potency"), it is more generally associated with the notion of potential.

The Ambiguity of "Power"

In relation to both the public and religious spheres, "power" is a highly ambiguous concept. In our contemporary world we face major problems with unhealthy and unbalanced "power" such as the use of violent force or the exploitation of unbalanced wealth. However, at the start of this essay, I want to acknowledge briefly the particular and painful ambiguities of Christian history regarding power.

Christianity has had particular difficulties, theoretical and practical, with giving priority to the way God's power is paradoxically revealed in the powerlessness of Jesus Christ's suffering and death. This speaks of God's love and the redemption of humankind. All too often, Christianity has focused on the image of the cross as sign of imperial power and military victory in the story of the Emperor Constantine. In 306 CE, Constantine was proclaimed the Western Roman Emperor but had to fight a civil war. This climaxed at the Battle of the Milvian Bridge (312 CE). It was said that, before the battle, Constantine saw a cross of light in the sky with the words "with this sign you will conquer." His troops then went on to victory with Christ's symbol on their shields.

Within decades, Christianity moved from being a persecuted minority to becoming the official religion of the empire. Unfortunately, it also took on many of the trappings of worldly "Constantinian" power, for example, in its hierarchical organization, the style of its buildings, and the wearing of imperial purple by senior clergy. Echoes of this culture survived into the modern era. Also, painfully, we cannot ignore the fact that the notorious sexual abuse crisis in Church contexts has undercurrents of power abuse. All of this sits uncomfortably with the radically different understanding of power expressed in the life and teachings of Jesus Christ.

My second brief example concerns Christianity's struggle with how to respond to Jesus's call to mission. The Greek New Testament, in its range of texts, does not offer a single definition of "mission." It highlights such things as broadly based witnessing to truth, living in loving fellowship, caring for people in need, and ministering—like Jesus—to the despised outsider. However, the so-called Great Commission in the Gospel of Matthew (28:19–20) became a favored text to legitimize active proselytizing by Christianity.[1] In this passage the risen Jesus appears to his disciples and commissions them with the words, "All authority in heaven and on earth has been given to me. Go therefore and make disciples of all nations, baptizing them in the name of the Father and of the Son and of the Holy Spirit, and teaching them to obey everything that I have commanded you."

Thus, across the centuries, "mission" came to imply an organized effort to spread Christianity. In some cases, this became intertwined with Western colonialism. We only have to think of the violent medieval wars, known as the Crusades, to "recover" the Holy Land, especially Jerusalem, which also led to the foundation of colonies in modern-day Turkey, Syria, Lebanon, and the Kingdom of Jerusalem. The Christian mission also became closely associated with European colonial power after the 1492 voyage of Columbus to the Americas. Although the motivation for Western colonialism was essentially commercial or political power, we cannot escape the fact that Christianity built on this imperial power-base. While much of the work of the Christian churches was humanitarian, some of it also involved robust and even enforced conversion.

After this ambiguous beginning, I now want to explore how "power" is understood in more constructive ways in some profoundly challenging Hebrew and Christian scriptures.

The Power of God

The foundation for all approaches to power in the Hebrew scriptures (the Old Testament in the Christian Bible) and the New Testament is how God's power is understood. God's power is first manifested as Creator. God is the origin of everything that exists. In Genesis 1, God commands and it happens. Genesis 1:3 records that "God said 'Let there be light and there was light.'" In 1:24, "God said, 'Let the earth bring forth living creatures of every kind.' . . . And it was so." The climax (verse 27) is the creation of humankind, described as "in the image of God."

This theme of God's power in creation appears many times in the Old Testament. For example, in Jeremiah 32:17 the prophet Jeremiah prays, "Ah Lord God! It is you who made the heavens and the earth by your great power and by your outstretched arm!" In Psalm 33, verse 6 affirms, "By the word of the Lord the heavens were made, and all their host by the breath of his mouth," and verses 8–9 add, "Let all the earth fear the LORD; let all the inhabitants of the world stand in awe of him. For he spoke, and it came to be; he commanded, and it stood firm." Interestingly, Psalm 115:3 bluntly states, "Our God is in the heavens; he does whatever he pleases." The wider context makes it clear that "whatever he pleases" is not an arbitrary exercise of power but is simply a reminder that nothing is beyond God's capacity.

Beyond the act of creation, in the Hebrew scriptures God's power is portrayed as lordship and as limitless. For example, Exodus 7–12 records God's liberation of the Israelites from slavery in Egypt. God's infinite power overcomes Pharaoh's limited power through ten plagues. One plague is darkness, which may refer to Egyptian sun worship and thus to the supremacy of God's power over the deities of Egypt. The LORD God says to Moses, "The Egyptians shall know that I am the Lord, when I stretch out my hand against Egypt and bring the Israelites out from among them" (Exod. 7:5). Indeed, the result is that Pharaoh cannot get rid of the Israelites fast enough! He says to Moses, "Rise up, go away from my people, both you and the Israelites!" (Exod. 12:31).

The infinite power of God to bring about what is good also appears in the New Testament. For example, in Matthew 19, Jesus proclaims that it will be hard for those with riches to enter the kingdom of heaven. The disciples ask, "Then who can be saved?" Matthew 19:26 affirms: "But Jesus looked at them and said, 'For mortals it is impossible, but for God all things are possible.'"

God's Power in the Life and Actions of Jesus Christ

For Christians, the life and actions of Jesus offer both a privileged insight into the nature of God's power and a medium for this to operate in actual events. God's power is manifested in the supernatural actions attributed to Jesus, particularly the miracles he performs. Miracles were mainly physical healing (sometimes related to exorcism), resurrection of the dead, and control over nature. For example, in Luke 9:37–43, Jesus is confronted by a man whose only child is said to be possessed by an evil spirit that brings about physical convulsions. In response, "Jesus rebuked the unclean spirit, healed the boy, and gave him back to his father. And all were astounded at the greatness of God." The same story also appears in the Gospels of Mark and Matthew (see Matt. 17:14–21; Mark 9:14–20).

There is also the famous story of Jesus feeding a great crowd of more than five thousand people who had followed him on foot and who had nothing to eat at the end of the day (see Matt. 14:15–21 and parallels in other Gospels). When asked by Jesus, the disciples can provide only five loaves and two fish. It is said that Jesus "looked up to heaven, and blessed and broke the loaves, and gave them to the disciples, and the disciples gave them to the crowds." Miraculously, everyone was well fed, and what remained was enough to fill twelve baskets.

Jesus's exercise of power was also frequently controversial, as he broke religious rules and breached conventional boundaries. For example, on several occasions he angered the religious authorities by curing people on the Sabbath when Jews were supposed to refrain from work. An example is the incident of a man with a withered hand in Mark 3:1–6. Jesus also responded to the needs of people in Gentile (that is, non-Jewish) areas. Thus, in the district of Tyre and Sidon, he healed the daughter of a Canaanite woman (Matt. 15:21–28). There are also stories of Jesus forgiving sins as well as healing people physically. Thus, Jesus showed that he has power or "authority" (Greek, *exousia*) to forgive sins by healing a paralyzed man. "The power of the Lord [God] was with him [Jesus] to heal" (Luke 5:17 and parallels). When the paralyzed man was brought to Jesus, he first said, "Friend, your sins are forgiven you." This was seen as blasphemous by the religious authorities. "Who can forgive sins but God alone?" Jesus responds robustly by asking whether it is easier to forgive sins or to heal paralysis. "So that you may know that the Son of Man has authority on earth to forgive sins," Jesus then cures the man who proceeds to glorify God.

Power and the Cross of Jesus

Earlier I mentioned that God's power is paradoxically manifested in the powerlessness of Jesus's sufferings and death. Counterintuitively, in Christian scriptures the trial and crucifixion of Jesus becomes God's channel for the redemption of humanity. In his two letters to the Corinthians, Paul addresses this paradox of power in weakness. In 1 Corinthians 6:14, "God raised the Lord [from the dead] and will also raise us by his power." In 2 Corinthians 13:4, Paul asserts, "For he [Christ] was crucified in weakness, but lives by the power of God. For we are weak in him, but in dealing with you we will live with him by the power of God." In another letter from Paul's circle, a whole new "ecology" of power is expressed that has great potential for reshaping approaches to human power and politics.[2] The writer prays that God may give us wisdom so that we can know "what is the immeasurable greatness of his power for us who believe, according to the working of his great power" (Eph. 1:19). Further, "God put this power to work in Christ when he raised him from the dead and seated him at his right hand in the heavenly places" (Eph. 1:20). Importantly, it is clearly stated that the power of God working in Christ is above the power and authority that operates in human contexts. Finally, the writer again prays "that, according to the riches of his glory, he [God] may grant that you may be strengthened in your inner being with power through his Spirit" (Eph. 3:16).

In the final book of the New Testament, the apocalyptic book of Revelation, the writer has a vision of heaven with God seated on a throne (chapter 4). Near the throne is a scroll on which is written the unalterable, eternal purposes of God. Who can open it? Only a slaughtered Lamb (the image of the crucified Jesus) may do so. Then the angels surrounding God's throne cry out, "Worthy is the Lamb that was slaughtered to receive power and wealth and wisdom and might and honor and glory and blessing!" (Rev. 5:12).

Human Power in the Teachings of Jesus Christ

The teachings of Jesus Christ, and echoes of this in the Pauline letters, also offer some interesting guidelines about the positive and negative aspects of the human exercise of power. Two examples illustrate the point.

A particularly famous phrase is "Render unto Caesar the things that are Caesar's, and unto God the things that are God's"—or, in the modern translation I am using, "Give to the emperor the things that are the emperor's, and to God the things that are God's." This phrase and the associated narrative appear in all three synoptic Gospels (Mark 12:13–17; Matt. 22:15–22; Luke 20:20–26). The context is a group of people sent by the Jewish religious authorities to question and entrap Jesus. In the Gospels of Mark and Matthew, it is also noted that Herodians were in the group. Herodians were political followers of Herod Antipas, whose power derived from the Roman emperor. The question concerned whether it was lawful for Jews (and, by extension, early Christian readers of the Gospels) to pay taxes to the emperor. In response, Jesus asks his questioners whose image is on a coin. It is an image of the emperor (presumably Tiberius). So Jesus responds, "Give therefore to the emperor, ..." If it is the emperor's image, the coin belongs to the emperor. This phrase is widely quoted as summarizing the proper relationship between religious people and state power. However, this response is ambiguous. Is it a straightforward justification of political power?

An important key to interpreting this narrative is that Caesar is also dependent on God. True, the coin "belongs" to the emperor because it displays his image. By implication, civil taxes can be legitimate even in the context of a foreign regime governing Judaea. However, beyond this lies the much deeper fact that all human beings—Jews, Christians, and Romans, including the emperor—belong to God, whose image they bear. God's ultimate power outweighs contingent political power. God's rule is over all humans without exception, including Caesar. This is particularly significant as Roman coins referred to the emperor as divine. There may be an implication here that allegiance to Caesar is somehow dependent on Caesar's conformity to God's will. Additionally, Jesus's words contain a spiritual message suggesting that people should be as exact in serving God in God's terms as they are in serving the emperor in terms of political power.

A second example is Paul's letter to the Romans, the longest letter to an early Christian community. Chapter 13 has echoes of the Gospel narrative about taxes and civil power. For some Christians this has been a difficult passage. Paul apparently endorses civil power. Verse 1 suggests that "everyone" is to be subject to the governing authorities. Even if God is the source of all authority, obedience to civil authority may be a form of obedience to God. The relationship of humans to God is not limited to the religious sphere. Legitimate political authority can be God's instrument. Thus, Romans 13:4 suggests, "for it is God's servant for your good." Verses 6–7 mention taxes. It is acceptable to pay them because they are for the common good via the power of civil government, delegated by God.

All true power belongs to God. Appropriate human power is a particular participation in God's power. This confronts us with the challenging choice of using that power in the service of others or for self-promotion. In the person of Jesus, God reveals the power of love, which Jesus lives out in his suffering and death and by preaching a community of mutual service and care. In all four Gospels, the "power" of the kingdom of God is to replace the human tendency to exercise power as domination. "Power" is now to be shown in service of others, even if that means appearing not to be powerful.

The Power of Love

One of the most striking aspects of power in the Christian scriptures is its relationship to love. In John 3:16, God's action is solely related to love. "For God so loved the world that he gave his only Son, so that everyone who believes in him may not perish but have eternal life." Then, in the later narrative about the Last Supper that Jesus shares with his disciples before his arrest and death, there are several references to the centrality of love. For example, in John 13:34–35, Jesus teaches, "I give you a new commandment, that you love one another. Just as I have loved you, you also should love one another. By this everyone will know that you are my disciples, if you have love for one another." The same teaching appears in Paul's first letter to the Corinthians, where he writes, "If I speak in the tongues of mortals and of angels, but do not have love, I am a noisy gong or a clanging cymbal" (13:1). Then in his letter to the Galatians, Paul exhorts the Christian community, "For you were called to freedom, brothers and sisters; only do not use your freedom as an opportunity for self-indulgence, but through love become slaves to one another" (5:13).

In the famous Beatitudes, or blessings, that appear in the Gospels of Matthew (chapter 5) and Luke (chapter 6), those to whom Jesus refers as "blessed" are the "poor" (Luke) or "poor in spirit" (Matthew), the hungry, those who mourn or who weep now, the meek, those who hunger and thirst for righteousness, the merciful, the pure in heart, the peacemakers, and those who are persecuted for the sake of righteousness. These do not refer to people with conventional power but to those who are vulnerable or who work for others out of love. The values expressed in the Beatitudes are also present in Jesus's narrative of the last judgment in Matthew 25:31–36. What distinguishes those who will inherit eternal life from those who are turned away is whether they served the needy and welcomed the stranger in this present life—for in these vulnerable people God was present. It is worth recalling that a "stranger" in the Hebrew and Christian scriptures is not simply someone who is not our kin. "The stranger" also embraces those who are outsiders, who are actively despised or excluded. This is presented in a particularly graphic way in the parable of the Good Samaritan in the Gospel of Luke (chapter 10). A lawyer confronts Jesus about his definition of "neighbor" when he teaches about the obligation in Jewish law to love both God and neighbor "as yourself." Jesus responds with a story in which a man is attacked by robbers on the road and left to die. Two Jewish officials, a priest and a Levite, both of them people of religious power, pass by, ignore the victim, and do nothing. Shockingly, the person who acts as a true neighbor by helping the victim is a Samaritan—that is, a member of a despised and outcast religious group in relation to orthodox Judaism.

God and the Re-Empowerment of the Poor

Up to this point, I have focused on biblical material. However, I want to end with a postscriptural example of reflections on power by the famous Peruvian liberation theologian Gustavo Gutiérrez. Gutiérrez uses scripture as his main theological resource and makes spirituality the cornerstone of his theology of God's presence "in all things." In one of his books, *We Drink from Our Own Wells: The Spiritual Journey of a People,* Gutiérrez links the "heroic" Christian practice of seeking to transform the world to following Christ even to the point of death.[3] Through God's unique power, life proclaims its final victory over death in Christ's resurrection. Gutiérrez also makes Christian discipleship the path of a *whole people* rather than of freestanding individuals. Here he draws on the book of Exodus and its narrative of God leading the people of Israel from slavery in Egypt via the wilderness to their eventual arrival in the land of promise. The Exodus image enables Gutiérrez to portray God's power as initiating everything and as the liberating force for the re-empowerment of the powerless.

In another book, *On Job: God-Talk and the Suffering of the Innocent*, Gutiérrez offers a creative commentary on the book of Job.[4] The suffering of Job becomes not only an example of the suffering of the innocent but also a representation of the search for God's justice. Job confronts God and discovers that his destiny ultimately depends on God's power. Job is drawn into a contemplative encounter with God and is empowered to abandon himself into God's love. He is shown a glimpse of God that takes him beyond simplistic human understandings of power and justice.

In summary, Gutiérrez suggests that the dominant economic, cultural, and political power systems in our world tend to make themselves into idols that dominate us spiritually as well as socially. Worship the system and worship the power that keeps the system in place! In contrast, the Christian approach to power, expressed in the person of Jesus Christ, seeks to redeem human history by placing God's liberating power at the heart of everything.

Conclusion

At the beginning of this essay I mentioned that we exist in a world in which the human use of power—political, economic, and religious—is frequently dysfunctional as it operates through domination and reinforces division. In contrast, the biblical foundations of Christianity offer a radically different vision. The annual meeting of Christian and Muslim scholars for which this essay was first prepared is entitled "Building Bridges." This title affirms the vital importance of breaking down the walls of separation that divide humanity and sometimes lead to destructive conflict that does not reflect the loving creativity of God.

Notes

1. All scriptural quotations are from the New Revised Standard Version of the Bible.

2. By "circle" I mean people closely associated with Paul. While the Letter to the Ephesians was traditionally attributed to Paul, some modern scholars judge that it may not have been written by Paul himself but by one of his followers.

3. See Gustavo Gutiérrez, *We Drink from Our Own Wells: The Spiritual Journey of a People*, trans. Matthew J. O'Connell (Maryknoll, NY: Orbis Books, 2003).

4. See Gustavo Gutiérrez, *On Job: God-Talk and the Suffering of the Innocent*, trans. Matthew J. O'Connell (Maryknoll, NY: Orbis Books, 1998).

PART TWO

The Theme of "Power" in Muslim and Christian Scriptures

The Contours of God's Power

An Introduction to Passages from the Qur'an and Hadith

MARTIN NGUYEN

The Question of Divine Power

Identifying passages from the Qur'an and hadith that help to delineate the nature of God's power and authority is a difficult task. A large part of this difficulty is deciding upon precisely where to begin. How does one define the idea of power within the Islamic tradition? For instance, I could have easily restricted myself to references to God's attribute of power (*qudra*) or capacity (*qadar*) as defined and centrally elevated by certain classical schools of Islamic theology, like the Ash'aris and Maturidis. After all, there are several scriptural passages that refer to God as *al-qadir*, a divine name that can mean God the Almighty, the all-powerful, or the omnipotent. While scriptural declarations like these are helpful, they reveal only a part of what we might imagine the "power" of God to be.

Divine power, I argue, is more than a measure of or, rather, the immeasurability of God's capacity or ability to create, shape, or direct creation. It is most certainly more than the exercise of force. Esteemed scholar Fazlur Rahman (d. 1988) captures the difficulty that many face when approaching the question of God's power as disclosed through the Qur'an. He writes,

> The immediate impression from a cursory reading of the Qur'ān is that of the infinite majesty of God and His equally infinite mercy, although many a Western scholar (through a combination of ignorance and prejudice) has depicted the Qur'ānic God as a concentrate of pure power, even as brute power—indeed, as a capricious tyrant. The Qur'ān, of course, speaks of God in so many different contexts and so frequently that unless all the statements are interiorized into a total mental picture—without, as far as

possible, the interference of any subjective and wishful thinking—it would be extremely difficult, if not outright impossible, to do justice to the Qur'ānic concept of God."[1]

There are two points worth underscoring. First, as Rahman admonishes, our conception of God's power should not be reduced to physical force, intimidation, or compulsion, as one might associate with earthly despots. It would be a misstep to prime one's gaze for signs of terribleness, malevolence, or caprice. Rather, Rahman argues, majesty and mercy more aptly characterize the power of God Almighty, a power that finds expression through forgiveness, forbearance, and magnanimity.

Second, Rahman cautions, God and God's power are not found in some verses while absent in others. Rather, the entirety of the Qur'an, from its first verse to its last, points us to many different dimensions of God's power. The Qur'an must be read holistically, not atomistically. Given these important caveats, then, where ought one to begin? The selection I have identified here is my modest attempt to find a beginning, but I do not want to give the impression that the passages that I have selected are all that there is to say. The selection is better understood as representing an entry point for engaging the set of questions concerning God's power.

Lastly, I understand Rahman to be signaling something greater, namely, that the totality of the Qur'an itself is an expression of and a testament to God's power. This is a point that I believe the Anglican bishop and scholar of Islam Kenneth Cragg (d. 2012) intended with his book *The Event of the Qur'an*. In Cragg's estimation, "The Qur'ān is a fusion, unique in history, of personal charisma, literary fascination, corporate possession, and imperative religion."[2] From a theological vantage, the Qur'an is the speech of God, *kalam Allah* (Q. 9:6; 48:15), and as such marks a phenomenal rupture in human existence. The "event" of the Qur'an, then, is an incision, if not an intervention, into the course of human history. Its message radically challenges our notions of reality. Its words radically refigure the grammar of everyday life. For those who heed its call, the Qur'an, as the word of God, exerts upon them a gravitational force. It is not merely a communication but a catalyst or a force for transformation. The event of the Qur'an overturns the familiar and conventional. It reveals the seen and the unseen, life after death, and a worldly end and a resurrection.

Rather than grapple with the event of the Qur'an and how God acts through its perpetual unfolding, we must more modestly begin by wrestling with select passages that more bluntly address the question of God's power, especially as it manifests in and through creation and more specifically in and through humankind. The selection presented here, divided across two sections, is my attempt to deliver a manageable compromise in which I hope to bring attention to interpretive tensions related to the power of God.

Dominion, Creation, and Anthropocentrism in Islamic Scripture

With respect to God's dominion and creation, I begin with what may seem an unconventional place and unconventional time. It is 1807, and a Muslim in his late thirties by the name of 'Umar b. Sayyid (d. 1864), who is a man of religious learning, has been captured and sold into slavery in Futa Toro, a region along the banks of the Senegal River. 'Umar b. Sayyid had been tragically drawn into the human driven machinery that was the transatlantic slave trade. Surviving an arduous and unforgiving journey across the dark waters of the Atlantic, he arrives in Charleston, South Carolina, to be sold into bondage. While his life from there on would continue to take arresting and unexpected turns—he ostensibly converts to Christianity in 1820, for example—'Umar b. Sayyid would spend the remainder of his life, nearly five and half decades, as a slave on the plantations of the Carolinas, never to escape bondage and never to see his home again.

Compelling as this narrative may be, what does the life of an enslaved Muslim have to do with the question of God's power in the Qur'an? I am recalling the life of 'Umar b. Sayyid because he left behind a set of written documents, including an autobiography, in which the Qur'an prominently appears, specifically Surat al-Mulk (67), the first passage among the scriptural texts for this essay. In fact, Surat al-Mulk figures in two distinct places in 'Umar b. Sayyid's extant corpus of writings. In 1819 'Umar b. Sayyid composed a letter aimed at a local Christian congregation in which he sought their aid in affecting his return to his home in Africa.[3] Notably, this letter, like all the others, was written in Arabic to an English-speaking congregation completely unfamiliar with the language. The historian John Hunwick, who has studied the letter, comments, "Perhaps the fact that they cannot read what he writes is of no great importance. It is rather the inherent *power* of the words themselves that is of significance."[4] And what precisely did these words say? His letter consists primarily of quotations from Islamic scripture: prophetic sayings and Qur'anic verses. 'Umar b. Sayyid is letting the words of God express his condition and desires. Indeed, he ends his letter dramatically, if not emphatically, with the verses of Surat al-Mulk.[5]

Then, in 1831, more than a decade later, 'Umar b. Sayyid wrote an autobiography in which he returns to Surat al-Mulk. This time, however, he opens his life narrative by reproducing from memory the entirety of the chapter from the Qur'an.[6] The choice of Surat al-Mulk is not insignificant. This chapter opens with a declaration that God alone possesses dominion (*mulk*) and that God is All-Powerful or omnipotent (*qadir*) (Q. 67:1). The potency of the scriptural invocation is all the more compelling when it is read against his condition of slavery, as a human being who is being forcefully subjugated to the will of another. It is for these reasons that Surat al-Mulk leapt to mind as a fitting passage with which to initiate the readings on the Qur'anic discourse of power. I believe these textual instances exemplify how the Qur'an was witnessed and experienced as an ongoing, unfolding, engaged event in the specificities of a lived, historical context. Surat al-Mulk gave voice to the religious imagination of an early Muslim in America thrust into the "New World's" unforgiving matrix of racial divisiveness.[7]

This sura from the Qur'an is also incredibly relevant because it presents a microcosm of the tensions that the remaining passages of the present selection address. After the proclamation of God's power made at the beginning, the chapter goes on to discuss various aspects of existence insofar as they are manifestations or signs of God's creative power. Our attention is drawn to life and death, the heavens and the earth, the waters coursing through them, and the birds in the sky above. Each aspect of nature is a testament to God's power and dominion. As the French Dominican Jacques Jomier notes, "Creation appears as the most characteristic manifestation of [God's] His power and His goodness."[8] The framing, however, is notably anthropocentric. The reader is reminded repeatedly and consistently of the benefits that human beings derive from God's creation. God did not merely bring these things into existence. God brings them into existence in an order pertinent to human life and well-being. Creation is described in such a way as to show how humanity is enmeshed into the larger system of God's creation. The nature of God's power in this sura is also connected to God's omniscience, His all-encompassing knowledge. God knows all that is uttered and held in the heart. Furthermore, an economy of salvation is also expressed. The reader or listener is made aware of a time to come in which recompense is meted out to the wicked condemned and the righteous saved. Notably, all of these points are framed as generalities.

Verse 28 refers to how God acts in the world with individual specificity. "Say, 'Have you considered whether God destroys me and those with me or has mercy upon us? Who will protect the disbelievers from a painful punishment?'" (Q. 67:28). This verse describes the ways in which God operates. God exercises His power for His prophets and those of faith and wields it punishingly against those who deny and disobey. Consider, then, how this sentiment measures against God's compassion, which follows immediately afterward.

After Surat al-Mulk, I would turn our attention to Surat al-Baqara [2]:255 because it is invoked in the lived realities of the everyday faithful. Though lengthy, it is one of the most well-known verses of the Qur'an because many Muslims across the world, Arabic-speaking and otherwise, commit it to memory in order to recite it whenever God's power of protection is sought. It functions as a talismanic invocation, which is a dimension of the Qur'an that should not be omitted. As to its content, verse 2:255 is known famously as *ayat al-kursi*, commonly translated as the Throne Verse or Pedestal Verse. It earns this name from the *kursi* mentioned therein, variously understood as a footstool or throne, hence representing the "seat" of God's power. It is a symbol that plays upon the image of God as sovereign or king.

Next, Surat al-Nahl [16]:40 deserves consideration for its conveyance of God's power personified in the command *kun*, the imperative form of the Arabic verb "to be." The phrase *kun fa-yakun*, or " 'Be!' And it is," powerfully expresses the facility with which God brings creation into existence.[9] With it, three more passages direct our attention to how God's power manifests through and within creation. I am not, however, addressing human power per se but rather how God's power maps between God, human creatures, and nonhuman creatures. Surat al-Aʿraf [7]:54–58 discloses to us how easily God summons and arranges creation. He creates the heavens and the earth in six days before mounting that repeated symbol of divine dominion, the *ʿarsh* or the throne. The revivification of vegetation upon dead earth, ostensibly a process of the perceived natural order, is likened to the resurrection of dead bodies, perceived to be more astounding and unfathomable, yet both are easy for God. God may stand above all of creation, so to speak, but are there relationships of power or structural differences woven into the created cosmos? In this same passage we are told the sun, moon, and stars are made subservient (*musakhkharat*) by God's command (*bi-amrihi*), but subservient to whom?[10]

The first seventeen verses of Surat al-Nahl might provide an answer since the language there is more explicit: night and day have been made subservient to humankind (*sakhkhara lakum*). Similar language is used for beasts of burden, such as cattle, horses, mules, and asses; the life of the sea; the waters sent down from the sky; and the mountains of the earth. What does this subservience entail when humans do not control the cycles or measures of these celestial and earthly phenomena? Human beings may benefit and make use of them, but do they actually control them. Do humans have *any* measure of power over them? And if so, how might that power be shared with God's power or derived from it?

The beginning of Surat al-Nahl also returns us to the issue of anthropocentrism. While the passage exemplifies anthropocentrism, by which I mean God is clearly speaking to human beings through the Qur'an, does God's illustration of the contours of divine power against various aspects of lived human existence necessarily imply an absolute hierarchical structure to creation or is the divine disclosure merely perspectival and not indicative of a natural order? In other words, does the Qur'an claim the superiority of humankind over other creatures, or is its language relative to its audience? Imagine, for example, God's message to the bees, referenced later in this *sura* (though not in the selected passages). If we human beings were privy to the fullness of God's revelation to the bees, "And thy Lord revealed unto the bee . . ." (Q. 16:69), might that revelation not seem anthophila-centric?[11] Would not that revelation seem to have little to do with humans and everything to do with bees? Moreover, would that revelation appear to imply the ascendancy of beekind over other aspects of creation? The question may seem frivolous, but it brings into relief, I believe, the issues at stake concerning the Qur'an's anthropocentrism. Do these verses actually represent a structural power relationship within creation established by God, or are these verses merely a perspectivally pinned, relativistic description of the human being's relational positionality within the system of creation?

Finally, Surat al-Fatir [35]:38–41 leads us to one more consideration concerning the dynamics of God's power in creation. In verse 39, God reminds us that He has appointed us, humankind, as vicegerents upon the earth (*khalaʾif fiʾl-ʿard*). What does it mean to be God's vicegerent or steward when we are told two verses later, "Truly God maintains the heavens and the earth, lest they fall apart. And were they to fall apart, none would maintain them after Him" (Q. 35:41)? What then is the purpose, scope, and efficacy of our human vicegerency when God seems so viscerally engaged in and critical to the affairs of creation?

These interpretive tensions are not posed so that we might resolve them but to prompt our reflection and offer direction to our conversation. As Fazlur Rahman states, "It is by meditating on creation that the Qurʾān invites man to rise towards God."[12] It is my hope that these trajectories of reflection and these selected passages will bring the reader a measure closer to understanding the nature of divine power within the folds of creation.

The Power of God in the World: Divine Action, Decree, and Intervention in Islamic Scripture

A dramatic encounter between God and Moses is briefly but vividly described in one of the narratives in the Qurʾan's Surat al-Aʿraf:

> And when Moses came to Our appointed meeting and his Lord spoke unto him, he said, "My Lord, show me, that I may look upon Thee." He said, "Thou shalt not see Me; but look upon the mountain: if it remains firm in its place, then thou wilt see Me." And when his Lord manifested Himself to the mountain, He made it crumble to dust, and Moses fell down in a swoon. And when he recovered, he said, "Glory be to Thee! I turn unto Thee in repentance, and I am the first of the believers." (Q. 7:143)

When Moses beseeches to behold God directly, God instead directs His servant's attention to the mountain before them. The mountain, a symbol of solidity, stability, and immensity upon the earth, is brought to ruin before the Creator's self-disclosure. Moses, although viewing the disclosure only secondarily, still collapses into unconsciousness. The story reveals how the power of God often works in the world: it precipitates a condition of overwhelmingness. The story is also important for the present section because it illustrates and accentuates the disparity that lies between the power and capacity of God and the power and capacity of created things. If mountains and prophets crumble before the Divine, how do mere human beings measure?

With this question in mind, we turn to take a closer look at scriptural passages from the tradition of Islam that focus more decidedly on the affairs of the human, specifically the concrete ways in which God's power is manifest in human life and where God seems to intervene decisively. "Intervention," of course, is a matter of perspective. Within Islam, the eternal God is always active and present in existence. I have selected passages where the perceived actions of God appear more consequential, by which I mean God's power seems complicit in human suffering, death, and condemnation. These are actions that may be interpreted from a human perspective as unforgiving, wrathful, spiteful, or heavy-handed, although that may not actually be the case from the divine perspective. The interpretative tension within the verses selected here revolves around scriptural statements that seem to assert divine determinism, omniscience, and omnipotence against statements that seem to recognize the vicissitudes of the human condition, that our state of mind changes, that our dispositions are malleable, that we possess agency and are accountable for the free choices that we make. How do we reconcile these two currents in the text?

The recently departed Qur'an scholar Andrew Rippin (d. 2016) provides a useful framework for parsing out the God-human relationship in the selected scriptural passages that follow. In an insightful chapter on God in the *Blackwell Companion to the Quran*, Rippin identifies "three major ranges of symbolism used in talking of God in the Qur'ān: the divine warrior-king, the divine judge, and the divine covenantor: that is . . . king:subject, judge:litigant, and master:servant."[13] While these relationships are not entirely independent of one another, each on its own helps to delineate important aspects of how the Qur'an is presenting the God-human discourse. The king-subject symbolic paradigm is identifiable in several of the passages discussed in the preceding section. It is implicit in the opening of Surat al-Mulk [67]:1 and the beginning of Surat al-Nahl [16]:1–2. It is explicit in *ayat al-kursi* (Q. 2:255) through the invocation of the *kursi*, the throne or pedestal of God. For the purposes of exploring divine action and divine decree in the present section, the language of covenant is of central importance.

The master-servant covenantal relationship is at the heart of Q. 7:172. Numerous Muslim sages and theologians recognize this verse as delineating a primordial covenant in which God asks, "Am I not your Lord?" (Q. 7:172) and to which preexistent humanity collectively responds, "Yea, we bear witness" (Q. 7:172).[14] The language covenant is most apparent in the final part of the exchange: "lest you should say on the Day of Resurrection, 'Truly of this we were heedless.'" (Q. 7:172). A covenant, however, implies the possibility of its violation. After all, what good is such an agreement if the possibility of or even desire for its violation does not exist? Indeed, the Qur'an implies, some among humanity will break it. What does this mean, then, for God's power? What is God's objective in establishing a covenant if all cannot or will not keep true to it?

Two passages—Surat al-Tawba [9]:51 and Surat al-Ḥadid [57]:22–24 turn our attention to the issue of God's decree. Both passages emphatically clarify that nothing befalls a person or the earth itself except by God's determination. Verses like these were relevant to advocates of Occasionalism, a doctrinal position held by certain theological schools like the Ash'aris, in that they were cited to assert that the omnipotent God is the efficient cause of all things.[15] In other words, causality does not exist. Yet, if God determines all events, how can human beings be held accountable?

Surat al-Baqara [2]:286 shows concern for the human side of the same issue: first, a person is not burdened beyond that of which she is capable, and the recompense of her actions, even if determined ontologically by God, is acquired or earned by the human being by virtue of the choice made. And so, second, this verse is also used in some theological circles as a support for the accompanying doctrine of acquisition, *kasb*, to assert that although the human being has no efficient power, he acquires the responsibility of an action because of the free choice that is made.[16] Free choice is what makes the reward or punishment "earned." And if a third count may be added, this is another example of a verse that finds life outside of textual interpretation in that it also serves as a supplicatory prayer recited by the faithful. The first part of the verse describes what God has established for a person, while the second part is the supplicatory human entreaties with respect to God's general decree.

The supposed tension, however, is not as stark as it would seem. Recall Rahman's understanding of a God that is ultimately compassionate. God's decree is not a mechanistic calculation of deeds and intentions. As attested by Surat al-Zumar [39]:53–54 and the prophetic saying from *Ṣaḥiḥ al-Bukhari* in which God states, "My Mercy overcomes My Wrath," God works with a substantial share of compassion and mercy. The question remains: How precisely does divine mercy function? Is God's mercy at play only prior to one's death, as possibly implied by the verse "whereafter . . . you will not be helped" (Q. 39:54), or is it part of the larger eschatological drama of judgment and accounting?

It is useful now to look at three Qur'anic passages (Q. 8:20–25; 2:6–20; 6:25) that speak of God sealing and covering hearts and taking away hearing and sight such that one falls into disobedient obstinacy. What does it mean that God comes between a person and her heart? Is the dissonance in the heart or is it that the heart requires the intervention of God so that it may be beneficially changed? In Surat al-Baqara [2]:6–20, God's role appears more vindictive than merely the sealing of hearts. We find God increasing people in disease, mocking them, and taking away their light. The historical context here is important. God is addressing a vulnerable Muslim community that has endured escalating and lethal hostilities for more than a decade by this time. His address may well be attuned to the fraught circumstances of that period. Nonetheless, latter-day readers must wrestle with how this eternal message speaks beyond the specificities of that historical moment. In Surat al-An'am, what is of special interest is the statement that certain disbelievers, "were they to see every sign, they would not believe in it" (Q. 6:25). What does this say about the signs themselves and their impotence in this case, or of the capacity of the human will to overcome all the signs of God? Then, with Surat al-Faṭir [35]:8, God speaks of evil deeds having been made to seem fair. The immediate questions that arise are made fair by whom and for what purpose if condemnation to the hellfire is the result?

Two Qur'anic passages turn to another related matter, namely, God's work in human history. Surat al-Hud [11]:116–20 provides a summation of God's modus operandi when faced with pervasive human disobedience. It draws attention to the long historical precedent of God's punishment, ruination, and destruction of past faithless communities, but, as Surat al-Hud seeks to affirm, these actions were deserved. While Surat al-Aʿraf [7]:94–102 does work similar to the passage from Surat al-Hud, this passage falls in the middle of a lengthy record of transgressions committed against particular prophets and the subsequent ruination suffered by them. Prior to verses 94–102, we are reminded of the destruction of the peoples of Noah, Hud, Saliḥ, Lot, and Shuʿayb. This is followed by a detailed account of Moses's confrontation with Pharaoh and his Egyptian people. In some respects, the sura pivots on the central axis that verses 94–102 represent. It is also worth noting that the passage is also another instance of God sealing human hearts.

The selection of readings then ends with a hadith from *Ṣaḥiḥ Muslim*, which begins, "There is not one among you whose place in Paradise or the Fire has not already been determined." I find the language of the Prophet Muhammad through-out the hadith insightful because I believe his words seek to delineate how the tension between the omnipotent and omniscient divine perspective relates to the limited ken of the human individual and her agency. The hadith also presents a converse to the sealing of hearts that precede it and in fact ends with an embed-ded Qur'anic verse, "We shall ease his way unto ease" (Surat al-Layl [92]:7). God may seal hearts for some, but He eases the path for others.

When confronted with God's omniscience and omnipotence, on the one hand, and the agency afforded human beings, on the other, the theological traditions of Islam have formulated various responses to these supposed tensions in revela-tion, in some cases articulating what proponents believe to be a robust and effi-cacious reconciliation. The inheritors and participants of traditions must nevertheless continue to revisit these answers and the source of their queries to ensure that a tradition endures. These selected passages are offered here in the tumult of the present as an opportunity for faithful reflection and deliberation on the ways that Islamic scripture reveals how God's power unfolds within the world and how God's decree determines the shape of human lives.

Notes

In this essay, all quotations from the Qur'an are according to *The Study Quran: A New Translation and Commentary* by Seyyed Hossein Nasr and Caner K. Dagli. Copyright © 2015 by Seyyed Hossein Nasr. Reprinted by permission of HarperCollins Publishers.

1. Fazlur Rahman, *Major Themes of the Qur'ān* (Minneapolis: Bibliotheca Islamica, 1994), 1–2.

2. Kenneth Cragg, *The Event of the Qur'an: Islam in Its Scripture* (Oxford: Oneworld, 1994), 13.

3. The letter was addressed to Maj. John Owen, the brother of 'Umar b. Sayyid's slave master, James Owen. At this time, James Owen was serving as or had recently ended his service as one of North Carolina's congressional representatives (1817–19). John Hunwick, "'I Wish to Be Seen in Our Land Called Āfrikā': 'Umar b. Sayyid's Appeal to Be Released from Slavery (1819)," *Journal of Arabic and Islamic Studies* 5 (2003): 73, 77.

4. Emphasis added. Hunwick, 69.

5. As Hunwick notes, the manuscript ends abruptly in the middle of the Qur'anic passage, implying that the entirety of the sura was likely written out, despite the final page being no longer extant.

6. A reproduction of one of the Arabic manuscripts with facing English translation has been published by Ala Alryyes alongside a series of studies related to 'Umar b. Sayyid and his sociohistorical context. Omar Ibn Said, *A Muslim American Slave: The Life of Omar Ibn Said*, trans. and ed. Ala Alryyes (Madison: University of Wisconsin Press, 2011), 47–79.

7. I believe the reference doubly important if we also keep in mind the work initiated by Georgetown University president John DeGioia in 2015, with the convening of the Working Group on Slavery, Memory & Reconciliation; see http://slavery.georgetown.edu/report/.

8. Jacques Jomier, *The Great Themes of the Qur'an*, trans. Zoe Hersov (London: SCM Press, 1997), 25.

9. The choice of Q. 16:40 could have been otherwise since the phrase *kun fa-yakun* appears in other places in the Qur'an, though in slightly different contexts. Those other verses are Q. 2:117; 3:47; 3:59; 6:73; 19:35; 36:82; and 40:68.

10. Sarra Tlili provides a helpful exploration of the issue in both its Qur'anic context and in extra-Qur'anic literature. Sarra Tlili, *Animals in the Qur'an* (Cambridge: Cambridge University Press, 2012), 92–115.

11. While Tlili does not discuss the implications of revelation regarding bees in the Qur'an, she does furnish an overview of how classical Muslim exegetes understood their inclusion in the scripture. Tlili, 161–62.

12. Jomier, *The Great Themes of the Qur'an*, 25.

13. Andrew Rippin, "God," in *The Blackwell Companion to the Qur'ān*, ed. Andrew Rippin (Malden: Blackwell, 2006), 227.

14. Cf. al-Ṭabarī, *al-Jāmi' al-bayān 'an ta'wīl āy al-qur'ān*, ed. Maḥmūd Shākir (Beirut: Dār Iḥyā' al-Turāth al-'Arabī, 2001), 9:132–41; al-Tha'labī, *al-Kashf wa'l-bayān*, ed. Muḥammad b. 'Āshūr (Beirut: Dār Iḥyā' al-Turāth al-'Arabī, 2002), 4:302–3; Fakhr al-Dīn al-Rāzī, *al-Tafsīr al-kabīr aw-mafātīḥ al-ghayb*, ed. Muḥammad 'Alī Bayḍūn (Beirut: Dār al-Kutub al-'Ilmiyya, 2000), 15:38–44; and Ibn 'Ajība, *Baḥr al-madīd fī tafsīr al-qur'ān al-majīd*, ed. 'Umar Aḥmad al-Rāwī (Beirut: Dār al-Kutub al-'Ilmiyya, 2010), 2:412–14. For Qur'an commentaries in English, see Ibn Kathīr, *Tafsir Ibn Kathir* (Abridged), ed. Shaykh Safiur-Rahman al-Mubarakpuri (Riyadh: Darussalam, 2000), 4:200–203; and Nasr et al., *The Study Quran*, 466–69.

15. Daniel Gimaret, *Théories de l'acte humain en théologie musulmane* (Paris: J. Vrin, 1980), 122–28; Dominik Perler and Ulrich Rudolph, *Occasionalismus: Theorien der Kausalität im arabisch-islamischen und im europäischen Denken* (Göttingen: Vandenhoeck & Ruprecht, 2000), 28–62; and Sherman Jackson, *Islam and the Problem of Black Suffering* (Oxford: Oxford University Press, 2009), 76–78.

16. Louis Gardet, *Les grands problèmes de la théologie musulmane: Dieu et la destinée de l'homme* (Paris: J. Vrin, 1967), 60–64; Louis Gardet, "Kasb," *Encyclopaedia of Islam*, 2nd ed., ed. C. E. Bosworth, E. van Donzel, B. Lewis, and Ch. Pellat (Leiden: Brill, 1954–2009), 4:692–94; and Jackson, *Islam and the Problem of Black Suffering*, 86–91, 106–9.

The Qur'an and Hadith on God's Power

Islamic Texts for Dialogue

God's Power and Dominion and the Dynamics of Power in Creation

Surat al-Mulk [67]

In the name of God, the Compassionate, the Merciful
[1]Blessed is He in Whose Hand lies sovereignty, and He is Powerful over all things, [2]Who created death and life that He may try you as to which of you is most virtuous in deed, and He is the Mighty, the Forgiving, [3]Who created seven heavens one upon another; no disproportion dost thou see in the Merciful's creation. Cast thy sight again; dost thou see any flaw? [4]Then cast thy sight twice again; thy sight will return to thee humbled and wearied. [5]Truly We have adorned the lowest heaven with lamps and made them missiles against the satans; and We have prepared for them the punishment of the Blaze. [6]And for those who disbelieve in their Lord is the punishment of Hell. What an evil journey's end! [7]When they are cast therein, they will hear it blaring as it boils over, [8]well-nigh bursting with rage. Whenever a group is cast therein, its keepers ask them, "Did not a warner come unto you?" [9]They say, "Indeed, a warner came unto us, but we denied him and said, "God did not send anything down; you are in naught but great error.'" [10]They say, "Had we listened or had we understood, we would not be among the inhabitants of the Blaze." [11]Thus do they admit their sin; so away with the inhabitants of the Blaze! [12]Truly for those who fear their Lord unseen there shall be forgiveness and a great reward.

[13]Keep your speech secret or proclaim it; truly He knows what lies within breasts. [14]Does He Who created not know? He is the Subtle, the Aware. [15]He is the One Who made the earth tractable for you; so travel the open roads thereof and eat of His provision. And unto Him is the Resurrection. [16]Do you feel secure

that He Who is Heaven will not cause the earth to engulf you while it churns? [17]Or do you feel secure that He Who is in Heaven will not unleash a torrent of stones upon you? Soon shall you know how My warning is.

[18]And indeed those before them denied. How, then, was the change I wrought! [19]Have they not considered the birds above them, spreading and folding up [their wings]? None holds them save the Compassionate. Truly He sees all things. [20]Who is it that will be a host for you, who may help you, apart from the Compassionate? The disbelievers are naught but in delusion. [21]Who is it that will provide for you if He withholds His provision? Nay, but they persist in insolence and aversion. [22]Is one who walks with his face stooped down more guided, or one who walks upright upon a straight path?

[23]Say, "He it is Who brought you into being and endowed you with hearing, sight, and hearts. Little do you give thanks!" [24]Say, "He it is Who multiplied you upon the earth and unto Him shall you be gathered." [25]And they say, "When will this promise come to pass, if you are truthful?" [26]Say, "Knowledge lies with God alone, and I am only a clear warner." [27]And when they see it close at hand, the faces of those who disbelieved shall be stricken, and it shall be said, "This is that for which you called." [28]Say, "Have you considered whether God destroys me and those with me or has mercy upon us? Who will protect the disbelievers from a painful punishment?" [29]Say, "He is the Compassionate; we believe in Him and trust in Him, and you will soon know who is in manifest error." [30]Say, "Have you considered? Were your water to vanish into the ground, then who would bring you flowing water?"

Surat al-Baqara [2]:255

God, there is no god but He, the Living, the Self-Subsisting. Neither slumber overtakes Him nor sleep. Unto Him belongs whatsoever is in the heavens and whatsoever is on the earth. Who is there who may intercede with Him save by His leave? He knows that which is before them and that which is behind them. And they encompass nothing of His Knowledge, save what He wills. His Pedestal embraces the heavens and the earth. Protecting them tires Him not, and He is the Exalted, the Magnificent.

Surat al-Nahl [16]:40

And Our Word unto a thing, when We desire it, is only to say to it, "Be!" and it is.

Surat al-Aʿraf [7]:54–58

[54]Truly your Lord is God, Who created the heavens and the earth in six days, then mounted the Throne. He causes the night to cover the day, which pursues it

swiftly; and the sun, the moon, and the stars are made subservient by His Command. Do not creation and command belong to Him? Blessed is God, Lord of the worlds! [55]Call upon your Lord humbly and in secret. Truly He loves not the transgressor. [56]And work not corruption upon the earth after it has been set aright, but call upon Him in fear and in hope. Surely the Mercy of God is ever nigh unto the virtuous. [57]He it is Who sends the winds as glad tidings ahead of His Mercy, so that when they bear heavy-laden clouds, We may drive them toward a land that is dead, and send down water upon it, and thereby bring forth every kind of fruit. Thus shall We bring forth the dead, that haply you may remember. [58]As for the good land, its vegetation comes forth by the leave of its Lord. And as for the bad, it comes forth but sparsely. Thus do We vary the signs for a people who give thanks.

Surat al-Nahl [16]:1–17

In the name of God, the Compassionate, the Merciful

[1]The Command of God is coming, so seek not to hasten it. Glory be to Him and exalted is He above the partners they ascribe. [2]He sends down angels with the Spirit from His Command to whomsoever He will among His servants, "Give warning that there is no god but I, so reverence Me!" [3]He created the heavens and the earth in truth. Exalted is He above the partners they ascribe. [4]He created man from a drop, and behold, he is a manifest adversary. [5]And cattle has He created for you, in which there is warmth and [other] uses, and whereof you eat. [6]And in them there is beauty for you, when you bring them home, and when you take them out to pasture. [7]And they bear your burdens to a land you would never reach, save with great hardship to yourselves. Truly your Lord is Kind, Merciful. [8]And [He has created] horses, mules, and asses, that you may ride them, and as adornment, and He creates that which you know not. [9]And it is for God to show the way, for some of them lead astray. Had He willed, He would have guided you all together.

[10]He it is Who sends down water from the sky, from which you have drink, and from which comes forth vegetation wherewith you pasture your cattle. [11]Therewith He causes the crops to grow for you, and olives, and date palms, and grapevines, and every kind of fruit. Truly in that is a sign for a people who reflect. [12]He has made the night and the day subservient unto you, and the sun, and the moon, and the stars are subservient by His Command. Truly in that are signs for a people who understand. [13]And whatsoever He created for you on the earth of diverse hues—truly in this is a sign for a people who reflect. [14]He it is Who made the sea subservient, that you may eat fresh meat therefrom, and extract from it ornaments that you wear. You see the ships plowing through it, and [this is so] that you may seek His Bounty, and that haply you may give thanks. [15]And He cast firm mountains into the earth, lest it shake beneath you, and streams, and ways, that haply you may be guided, [16]and landmarks, and by

the stars they are guided. [17]Is He Who creates like one who creates not? Will you not, then, reflect?

Surat al-Fatir [35]:38–41

[38]Truly God knows the unseen of the heavens and the earth. Truly He knows what lies within breasts. [39]He it is Who appointed you vicegerents upon the earth. So whosoever disbelieves, his disbelief is to his detriment. The disbelief of the disbelievers increases them with their Lord in naught but odium. And the disbelief of the disbelievers increases them in naught but loss. [40]Say, "Have you considered your partners upon whom you call apart from God? Show me what they have created of the earth. Do they have a share in the heavens, or did We give them a book, such that they stand upon a clear proof from it?" Nay, the wrongdoers promise one another naught but delusion. [41]Truly God maintains the heavens and the earth, lest they fall apart. And were they to fall apart, none would maintain them after Him. Truly He is Clement, Forgiving.

Divine Action and Predeterminism

Surat al-Aʿraf [7]:172

And when thy Lord took from the Children of Adam, from their loins, their progeny and made them bear witness concerning themselves, "Am I not your Lord?" they said, "Yea, we bear witness"—lest you should say on the Day of Resurrection, "Truly of this we were heedless."

Surat al-Tawba [9]:51

Say, "Naught befalls us, save that which God has decreed for us. He is our Master, and in God let the believers trust."

Surat al-Hadid [57]:22–24

[22]No misfortune befalls the earth nor yourselves, save that it is in a Book before We bring it forth—truly that is easy for God—[23]that you not despair over what has passed you by, nor exult in that which has been given unto you. And God loves not any vainglorious boaster, [24]those who are miserly and enjoin people to be miserly. Yet whosoever turns away, truly God, He is the Self-Sufficient, the Praised.

Surat al-Baqara [2]:286

God tasks no soul beyond its capacity. It shall have what it has earned and be subject to what it has perpetrated. "Our Lord, take us not to task if we forget or err! Our Lord, lay not upon us a burden like Thou laid upon those before us. Our Lord, impose not upon us that which we have not the strength to bear! And pardon us, forgive us, and have mercy upon us! Thou art our Master, so help us against the disbelieving people."

Surat al-Zumar [39]:53–54

[53]Say, "O My servants who have been prodigal to the detriment of their own souls! Despair not of God's Mercy. Truly God forgives all sins. Truly He is the Forgiving, the Merciful. [54]Turn unto your Lord and submit to Him before the punishment comes upon you, whereupon you will not be helped."

Hadith

Sahih al-Bukhari: Kitab Bab' al-Khalq 59:5

Hurayra (may God be pleased with him) narrated that the Messenger of God (God's blessings and peace be upon him) said, "When God completed creation, He wrote in His Book which is with Him above His Throne, 'My Mercy overcomes My Wrath.'"

Surat al-Anfal [8]:20–25

[20]O you who believe! Obey God and His Messenger, and turn not away from him, even as you hear [him]. [21]And be not like those who say, "We hear," though they hear not. [22]Truly the worst of beasts in the sight of God are the deaf and the dumb who understand not. [23]Had God known of any good in them, He would have caused them to hear; yet had He caused them to hear, they would have turned away in rejection. [24]O you who believe! Respond to God and the Messenger when he calls you unto that which will give you life. And know that God comes between a man and his heart, and that unto Him shall you be gathered. [25]And be mindful of a trial that will not befall only those among you who do wrong; and know that God is severe in retribution.

Surat al-Baqara [2]:6–20

[6]Truly it is the same for the disbelievers whether thou warnest them or warnest them not; they do not believe. [7]God has sealed their hearts and their hearing. Upon their eyes is a covering, and theirs is a great punishment. [8]Among mankind are those who say, "We believe in God and in the Last Day," though they do not believe. [9]They would deceive God and the believers; yet they deceive none but themselves, though they are unaware. [10]In their hearts is a disease, and God has increased them in disease. Theirs is a painful punishment for having lied. [11]And when it is said unto them, "Do not work corruption upon the earth," they say,

"We are only working righteousness." [12]Nay, it is they who are the workers of corruption, though they are unaware. [13]When it is said unto them, "Believe as the people believe," they say, "Shall we believe as fools believe?" Nay, it is they who are the fools, though they know not. [14]And when they meet those who believe they say, "We believe," but when they are alone with their satans they say, "We are with you. We were only mocking." [15]God mocks them, and leaves them to wander confused in their rebellion. [16]It is they who have purchased error at the price of guidance. Their commerce has not brought them profit, and they are not rightly guided. [17]Their parable is that of one who kindled a fire, and when it lit up what was around him, God took away their light, and left them in darkness, unseeing. [18]Deaf, dumb, and blind, they return not. [19]Or a cloudburst from the sky, in which there is darkness, thunder, and lightning. They put their fingers in their ears against the thunderclaps, fearing death. And God encompasses the disbelievers. [20]The lightning all but snatches away their sight. Whenever it shines for them, they walk therein, and when darkness comes over them they halt. Had God willed, He would have taken away their hearing and their sight. Truly God is Powerful over all things.

Surat al-An'am [6]:25

Among them are those who listen to thee, but We have placed coverings over their hearts, such that they understand it not, and in their ears a deafness. Were they to see every sign, they would not believe in it, so that when they come to thee, they dispute with thee. Those who disbelieve say, "This is naught but fables of those of old."

Surat al-Fatir [35]:8

And what of the one, the evil of whose deeds has been made to seem fair to him, such that he thinks it beautiful? Truly God leads astray whomsoever He will and guides whomsoever He will; so let not thy soul be expended in regrets over them. Truly God knows that which they do.

Surat al-Hud [11]:116–120

[116]So why were there not among the generations before you those possessing merit, who would forbid corruption upon the earth, other than a few of those whom We saved among them? Those who did wrong pursued the luxuries they had been given, and they were guilty. [117]And thy Lord would never destroy the towns unjustly, while their people were reforming. [118]And had thy Lord willed, He would have made mankind one community. But they did not cease to differ, [119]save those upon whom thy Lord has Mercy—and for this He created them. And the Word of thy Lord is fulfilled: "I shall surely fill Hell with jinn and men altogether." [120]All that We recount unto thee of the stories of the messengers is

that whereby We make firm thine heart. And herein there has come unto thee the truth, and an exhortation and a reminder for the believers.

Surat al-A'raf [7]:94–102

[94]We sent no prophet to a town but that We seized its people with misfortune and hardship, that haply they would humble themselves. [95]Then We replaced evil [circumstances] with good, till they multiplied and said, "Hardship and ease visited our fathers [as well]." Then We seized them suddenly, while they were unaware. [96]Had the people of the towns believed and been reverent, We would surely have opened unto them blessings from Heaven and earth. But they denied, so We seized them for that which they used to earn. [97]Did the people of the towns feel secure from Our Might coming upon them by night, while they were sleeping?

[98]Or did the people of the towns feel secure from Our Might coming upon them in broad daylight, while they were playing? [99]Did they feel secure from God's plotting? None feels secure from God's plotting save the people who are losers. [100]Does it not serve as guidance unto those who inherited the earth after its [earlier] inhabitants that, if We willed, We could smite them for their sins and set a seal upon their hearts such that they would not hear? [101]These are the towns whose stories We have recounted unto thee. Their messengers certainly brought them clear proofs, but they would not believe in what they had denied earlier. Thus does God set a seal upon the hearts of the disbelievers. [102]We did not find most of them [faithful to their] pact. Indeed, We found most of them to be iniquitous.

Sahih Muslim: *Kitab al-Qadr 46:11*

Ali narrated that one day the Messenger of God (God's blessings and peace be upon him) was sitting with a stick in his hand with which he was scrawling upon the ground. He raised his head and said, "There is not one amongst you whose place in Paradise or the Fire has not already been determined." They said, "O Messenger of God, then, why should we perform good deeds? Should we not trust [in our predetermined fate]?" [The Messenger] said, "No, perform good deeds, for everyone will find the deeds for which he was created easy to do." Then he recited the verse: [5]"As for one who gives and is reverent, [6]and attests to what is most beautiful, [7]We shall ease his way unto ease" (Surat al-Layl [92]:5–7).

Note

Translations of the Qur'an provided here are according to *The Study Quran: A New Translation and Commentary* by Seyyed Hossein Nasr and Caner K. Dagli. Copyright © 2015 by Seyyed Hossein Nasr. Reprinted by permission of HarperCollins Publishers. Translations of the hadiths included in this chapter have been provided by members of the Seminar.

Biblical Conceptions of Power— Divine and Human

STEPHEN L. COOK

"Power," divine and human, has multiple dimensions in the texts of the Christian Bible, the combined Old and New Testaments. Both testaments assume that YHWH, as the one true God, is the Creator and Ruler of all things. God's divine prerogative relativizes all other exercises of power. At the same time, both testaments wrestle with unconventional and even paradoxical dimensions and aspects of the nature of divine power and its human corollaries.

Both testaments take up the ancient mythic and archetypal image of the Divine Warrior in portraying God's cosmic power. The Divine Warrior battles and defeats chaos, usually appearing in the guise of a sea monster. Order and Shalom emerge from God's victory. Yet the Bible contains little or no myth in pure form but rather mythic images co-opted and appropriated critically for theological ends. Several Old Testament texts use the Divine Warrior myth to portray the deep ontological significance of God's saving acts in history. Several New Testament texts reveal Jesus acting in the role of the Warrior, but as part of his humble earthly ministry.

Close examination of the biblical texts reveals key paradoxes repeatedly associated with divine and human power. The texts of Second Isaiah (Isaiah chapters 40–55) argue the mystery that human striving, especially religious exertion, is often foolish. True power derives from aligning with God's ways and with God's Word directing history.

In powerful poems about God's Suffering Servant, the paradoxical power of human vulnerability is revealed. The Servant's other-centered self-sacrifice turns out to be of amazingly transformative power. The New Testament portrays Jesus stepping into the ideal role of the protagonist of Isaiah's Servant Songs. Repeatedly, New Testament texts argue that Jesus's descent to death and rising to new life forms an extreme, paradigmatic witness to the mystery that selfless, sacrificial servanthood leads to victory, true power, and authority.

Psalm 29:1–11
The Coming of the "Divine Warrior"

The form and mythological imagery of Psalm 29 resemble early Canaanite poems, poetry from before Israel settled in Canaan. Indeed, the psalm sounds to scholars much like a poem written at Ugarit, a coastal city far north of Israel with a polytheistic, Bronze Age culture. In its Ugaritic context, the language of Psalm 29:1 refers not to angelic beings but to actual deities, "divine beings."[1] The various locales that Psalm 29 mentions—Lebanon (v. 5), Sirion (v. 6, the Phoenician name for Mount Hermon), and Kadesh (v. 8, a site on the Orontes River)—are to Israel's north, around the Lebanon Mountains.[2] Thus, Psalm 29 co-opts north-Semitic, Ugaritic-like mythology to portray the power of YHWH, the true God.

To its original audience in Israel, the psalm aimed fierce polemics at the Ugaritic and Canaanite storm-god, Baal. It names YHWH eighteen times, never once speaking of Baal. YHWH, not Baal, controls earth's fertility, fuels nature's fecundity. Employing the term "voice"/"thunder" a symbolic seven times, the psalm evokes notions of complete, sweeping power. Indeed, the word's relentless, tympanic repetition provokes awe at a power transcending human control, dwarfing mortal ability. That is why the psalm risks using mythological language. The artful diction shouts aloud that God's power is *transcendent*.

As God, in the guise of a tremendous storm, hurls lightning at the Mediterranean Sea and pounds the earth with rain, ancient readers recognized the ancient motif of the "Divine Warrior." In the role of the Divine Warrior, God overpowers "Sea," that is, primordial chaos. Then, God forms the world as an ordered, fertile realm. God thunders over ocean floods, over sea depths (v. 3), understood as eerie chaos. In verse 10, God sits victorious over the *mabbul*, the subdued floodwaters of creation time, the uncanny abyss of chaos.

God's battle with the ocean floods of chaos is not simply an event of creation. It is celebrated repeatedly in ritual (see Psalms 24:7–10; 46:8–11; 93). It is experienced historically in divine acts of saving intervention (see, e.g., Exod. 15:3; Josh. 10:11; Judg. 5:20; 1 Sam. 7:10). If violent warrior imagery seems offensive, remember that apocalyptic texts appropriate this very metaphor in describing the resurrection and God's end-time victory over evil.[3] When the Divine Warrior appears and defeats chaos, life revives from death (e.g., see Isa. 35:1–10).

Isaiah 55:6–11
God's Towering Transcendence and Irresistible Word

In what way does earth experience God's presence and power? Different traditions within the Bible answer this question differently. The texts of Isaiah 40–55, the prophetic poems known as "Second Isaiah," present the reader with a God of radical otherness, of towering transcendence. For reasons I explain elsewhere, I believe Second Isaiah's poems, including Isaiah 55:6–11, were composed between 550 and 539 BCE by a group of Aaronide priests living in Babylonian exile.[4] The exile, however, will soon end. God's pardon has come (55:6).

In this poetry, God's power to evoke the exiles' return and deliverance directly connects with God's eerie otherness. God's thoughts and ways are inscrutable, beyond human imagining (v. 8). The plans of God soar high above human plans, far from the reach of earthbound mortals (v. 9). The revelation is salvific since it pushes God's people to deflate the ego, making room for God's pardon. Demanding life on one's own terms, insisting on comprehension and control, is self-defeating. Acknowledging God's prerogative, feeling awe at God, empowers. Islam also envisions a link between God's power and generosity.

The poem's last stanza in verses 10 and 11 describes God's Word as a tangible force connecting heaven and earth. The world's creator, YHWH, stands outside the world but interacts with it directly and intentionally through creative utterance. God speaks new realities into history, changing its course, accomplishing God's purposes. Unlike in Islam, history is not itself God's will, but it does bow naturally to God's creative correction of its course. Verse 10's analogy between natural precipitation (rain and snow) and the creative workings of God is telling. God works gratuitously, apart from human striving, and with definitive, natural rhythms, which human beings can observe. To find deliverance and peace, humans should reverently align their lives with the determinative rhythms by which God creatively guides terrestrial existence. They should catch God's natural winds in their sails.

Isaiah 51:9–16
God's Power in Cosmogony, Exodus, and Liberation from Exile

Isaiah 51:9–16, like Psalm 29 (discussed above), co-opts and redeploys ancient mythological images known from Canaanite polytheism. It celebrates God's power, which it calls the "arm of the LORD" (v. 9), as the Divine Warrior's primordial defeat of the chaos dragon. God's power must certainly be of cosmic scope, since at the time of creation God famously dispatched the slithering chaos dragon, making mincemeat of Rahab (v. 9).

"Rahab," like Yam ("sea"; Job 7:12; 9:8), Leviathan (Job 3:8; Ps. 74:14; Isa. 27:1), Tohu/Tiamat (Gen. 1:2; Ps. 148:7), and Tannin ("dragon"; Job 7:12; Ps. 74:13; Isa. 27:1), is a name for the mythical sea monster, the disseminator of chaos and archenemy of the Divine Warrior. Tannin is a parallel name for Rahab in our text. Reflecting the restless crashing of the sea's waves, the name Rahab means "Surging One"/"Raging One." Job 9:13 refers to "the minions of Rahab—[that monster of the sea and purveyor of chaos]."[5] Job 26:12 declares that "by His power," God "stilled the sea, [quelling the chaos]"; "by His wisdom, He pierced Rahab, [evil of the sea]." Psalm 89:9–10 likewise extolls God's power, God's "mighty arm," by declaring, "When [violent] waves rise up, You still them. You defeated Rahab, [that ancient monster of chaos], and left it lifeless."

As with Psalm 29, Isaiah 51 appropriates mythic images critically. The aim is not to propagate mythic thinking but to broaden readers' imaginations about real life. The claim is that God's historical exercises of power have transcendent dimensions. Mythic images help reveal the transcendent depths of God's mighty acts. Verse 10 insists that the exodus from Egypt was no simple liberation of slaves but divine re-creation, giving humanity a new start. Verse 11 describes restoration from Babylonian exile as no mere political repatriation but as God refashioning existence. God's removal of "sorrow and sighing" suggests a new world without desperation and depression, perhaps a world without funerals and mourning.

In the present holistic shape of Isaiah's book, such a world was promised word-for-word in a context more than a century before any experience of Babylonian exile. Specifically, Isaiah 35:10 reveals the promise in a literary context preceding Second Isaiah, chapters 40–55. The book's "canonical" form thus corroborates how Isaiah 51 is about more than a political liberation around 539 BCE. It is about God's power to renew existence, a power that God has not yet fully exercised, even as of Isaiah 51. Isaiah 35:10 still awaits definitive fulfillment.

Isaiah 31:1–3
God's Cosmic Prerogative, Relativizing Political Strategies

Isaiah 31:1–3 is from pre-exilic Judah, from the eighth century BCE. In prophesying this word, Isaiah likely confronts King Hezekiah during a period of anxiety about Assyria's military threat. A date around 710 BCE, when Hezekiah was first fortifying Jerusalem (see Mic. 3:10) or in the years before the Assyrian crisis of 701 BCE, is likely. The Northern Kingdom had fallen to the Assyrians in 722 BCE, and Hezekiah was highly concerned that an Assyrian invasion of Judah was inevitable. He was pursuing military and political strategies, such as a military alliance with Egypt (see Isa. 20:5; 30:1–3). Other nations in Syria and Canaan joined him in seeking Pharaoh Shabako's help in creating a coalition against Assyria.

Hezekiah would have known Isaiah's position on his efforts. The prophet had earlier declared it to King Ahaz around 735 BCE. Isaiah had insisted that Ahaz trust God's promises to Zion, David's city and temple, not political and military solutions. Invoking archetypal images of the miracle rivers of Eden, Isaiah said that Ahaz and all Judah should trust in "the waters of Shiloah that flow gently" (Isa. 8:6). He reiterated the Zion theology of Psalm 46:4, 5, "There is a river whose streams make glad the city of God. . . . God is in the midst of the city; it shall not be moved; God will help it when the morning dawns."[6]

Of special interest is how Zion theology in Isaiah 31 turns common thinking about power on its head. Just like today's readers, Kings Ahaz and Hezekiah assumed that political-military force is that which is real and strong, whereas divine reality is spectral and wispy. Our passage upturns this thinking. Verse 3 insists that frail mortals and horses of flesh are the spectral realities, whereas the supernatural is what is solid and invincible. "These Egyptians are mere humans, not God! Their horses are puny flesh, not mighty spirits!"[7] Significantly, Islam has a tradition of not trusting in troop numbers and "horsepower."

Exodus 14:10–15:3
God's Classic Mighty Work at the Red Sea

God's parting of the Red Sea forms a focal point in biblical Israel's self-understanding. Indeed, the Old Testament story, in outline, may be viewed as an ellipse with two foci, the Red Sea event and the return from Babylonian exile. We saw in Isaiah 51 that these two mighty acts of God stand parallel to each other. In each, God acts with power in history to create a servant people that may become God's image on earth, bringing a new lifestyle to the world.

Modern scholars usually place the deliverance at the Red Sea near the end of the thirteenth century BCE. Our text in Exodus 14:10–15:3, however, represents a mosaic of literary strands composed much later, at various points in the monarchic era. The story of the deliverance was of such formative and theological moment that over time it was told and retold from different perspectives. Why was there such huge interpretive interest in this story? Apparently, many in Israel viewed it as God's paradigmatic redemptive mighty act, through which God called Israel as God's own. "Out of Egypt I called my son" (Hos. 11:1).

One of the strands in our passage, written by Aaronide priests, presents a unique dimension of God's exercise of power that modern readers often find troubling. Disturbingly, Exodus 14:17 has God direct the will and decision-making of the Egyptians in a manner that both complicates Israel's distress and ensures Egypt's doom. Is it possible to say anything meaningful about what may be going on here in this paradoxical exercise of divine power?

Some clues arise from the insights gained in our brief examination of Isaiah 55:6–11 above. There we saw the Aaronide priests present a God of radical otherness. The numinous eeriness of this God reappears in Exodus 14:17, when God actively promotes chaos (cf. Isa. 45:7). This is an "amoral" God, whose ways and thoughts are not at all like ours (Isa. 55:8). But just because the God of Exodus 14:17 is not a "practical" God does not mean the ultimate aim is not positive human transformation. No, the root problem behind Israel's Egyptian captivity was the arrogance of Pharaoh and his advisors. Earth's great need is to be rid of all such pretensions to security and control that keep life cold and brutish. For

God to "gain glory" (v. 17) is for God's preternatural otherness to shrink pride and allow people to find their true humanity, that is, to relinquish autonomy and become truly free as God's image.

Isaiah 52:13–53:3
God's Power Revealed Paradoxically in Suffering Servanthood

The paradox that God's ways and thoughts are not at all like ours (Isa. 55:8) is perhaps nowhere clearer than in the set of poems within Second Isaiah commonly termed the "Servant Songs."[8] The songs include Isaiah 42:1–4; 49:1–6; 50:4–11; and 52:13–53:12 (from which our text is excerpted). To these four texts I would add Isaiah 61:1–3 as well as some brief appearances of the Servant figure in Isaiah 48:16; 51:16; and 59:21. Scholars have long wrestled over the nature of these poems, their relationship to their context in Second Isaiah, and the identity of their ideal protagonist. Much ink has been spilled, but no consensus has emerged.

My own view is that the Servant protagonist of the poems is an ideal poetic figure partially modeled on Moses. For a brief focused time, the Servant takes up the true role and calling of the entire people of Israel and exhibits its model performance (see Isa. 49:3—"[God] said to me, 'You are [now] my servant, Israel'").[9] The poems of the Servant constitute a theological meditation on the power of Israel's ideal role of sacrificial servanthood. That the passage is about the nature of ultimate power is clear from Isaiah 53:1, which speaks of God's revelation of "the arm of the LORD." As we saw in Isaiah 51:9 (and Psalm 89:10), the "arm" represents the Divine Warrior's victorious might in defeating chaos. The paradox in Isaiah 53:1 is that this sort of overwhelming force is hard to see in the mission and work of a frail Suffering Servant. "Who has seen in *it* a revelation of Yahweh's arm?"[10]

How does the text understand divine power to manifest itself in the Servant's vulnerability? Part of the answer lies in the passage's deliberate echo of an earlier text in Isaiah's book. Isaiah 53:2 speaks of the Servant growing before God "like a young plant, . . . like a root out of dry ground." Readers familiar with Isaiah's texts hear a distinct resonance with the messianism of Isaiah 11:1–9.[11] Isaiah 11 speaks of a saving figure appearing on earth as a tender green shoot, springing up unexpectedly. The passage goes on to explain that the figure's rule does not revolve around ego and control but around reverence (vv. 2–3) and preferential treatment for the needy and poor, not the great (v. 4). In his peaceable kingdom, physical violence is extirpated (vv. 6–9). Indeed, the lamb will play host to the wolf (v. 6).

Here is an insight into the tremendous power of frailty and vulnerability. The Hebrew of Isaiah 11:6 refers specifically to the wolf living as a dependent, resident alien in the society of sheep. Peace on earth is achieved as the sheep relax their guard, drop their self-concern. Their nonviolent stance against possible wolf violence puts the wolves in a position where acts of aggression become highly problematic. Attacking their willing hosts would be entirely shameful. At the same time, the sheep's courage can only reflect awe and reverence before the LORD (11:9). Their resolve constitutes a supreme witness to God's mighty power to uphold the honor and life of God's servants despite all extremes (Isa. 53:10, 12). I am highly impressed with the Servant's willingness to adopt the nonviolent and power-laden witness of these sheep (Isa. 53:7). Islam also knows the powerful notion of nonviolent resistance.[12]

Hosea 11:1–9
God's Power and Vulnerability in Conflict

Hosea 11:1–9 presents a heartfelt monologue of God, who speaks as the "parent" of a wayward, obstinate "child." (On Israel as God's son, see Deut. 1:31; 8:5; 32:6; Jer. 2:14; 3:19, 22; 31:9, 20.) God's pained language here is juridical, inviting readers to imagine a distraught father pleading and debating with elders about his wicked child. Life with the son has been a trial. The son's rebelliousness and stubbornness have become so completely ingrained that they will inevitably pull him down. As the passage unfolds, it becomes clear that Israel's rebellious path will in fact be a journey through death to renewed life. Israel's unremitting recalcitrance subjects it to the law of Deuteronomy 21:18–21, which declares it subject to death by stoning!

Especially fascinating here is the intense conflict visible in the passage between God's fierce power to judge and God's inner agony at the thought of doing so. The poetry reveals a God of both tremendous might and, simultaneously, immense vulnerability. God's great power, it appears, is not enough to protect against the awful pain of Israel's rejection and downfall. God's heart is overwhelmed, torn apart. God's insides churn in protest at the thought of giving up on Israel. God can hardly bear to even think such thoughts (v. 8).

While human parents might bring themselves to turn over an impossibly reprobate heir to town elders for stoning, the God of Hosea, in mysterious divine otherness and freedom, recoils at the thought (v. 8). And although Israel eventually succumbs to catastrophic judgment in 722 BCE, even this, in God's will, is not the end. The people of God are graced to find a way through destruction. According to Hosea 11:10–11, God's people, though "stoned" to death, can look forward to a future "resurrection" experience.

Matthew 8:14–17
Jesus's Divine Power over Disease and Demons

Matthew 8:14–17 recounts a sample day in Jesus's ministry, highlighting his authoritative miracle-working activity. The passage is part of a larger section of Matthew, 8:1–9:34, devoted to the theme of authoritative healings. The setting is

Capernaum, the home of Jesus's disciple Peter. What starts as a single miraculous healing of Peter's mother's high fever escalates to include the healing of "all who were sick" in the village (v. 16). What is more, the healings include the exorcism of demons. Thus, the passage illustrates Jesus's divine power and prerogative over both disease and demons. It is notable that Jesus's mere "word" casts out spirits, just as God created the cosmos through a simple word (e.g., Gen. 1:3).

Discussion of demons often feels alien and superstitious to modern readers of the global north. Such dark, supramundane powers, however, were a part of biblical life and appear in various guises also in the Hebrew Bible (see Lev. 16:8, 10; Isa. 13:21; 34:14). At a minimum, Jesus's focus on casting them out of people's lives shows that the redemption he brings entails transcendent dimensions. His ministry is not merely about ethical persuasion and biological health but also confronts sickness and sin as enslaving "Powers" in existence.

Verse 17 concludes the passage by observing that Jesus's healing work fulfills a prophecy of Isaiah, Isaiah 53:4, part of the fourth Servant Song. Matthew's readers would be expected to be familiar with the citation's larger context, which characterizes the Servant as humble, sensitive, and allied with the needy. Jesus certainly steps into this ideal role, depicted poetically over four centuries earlier. But isn't Isaiah's Servant focused on sin, not disease (Isa. 53:5–6)? No, as the "arm of the LORD," the Servant defeats all chaos, including disease and demonic oppression. Thus, in Ugaritic myth, the divine warrior Baal leads supernatural healers known as Rapiuma to intervene on earth, healing diseases and repelling evil.

Matthew 8:18–27
Jesus's Cosmic and Apocalyptic Power over Chaos

Our next passage, enacted right after the events in Capernaum, presents an even sharper picture of Jesus as the Divine Warrior. As Jesus's group prepares to cross the Sea of Galilee, the scene is set for a confrontation with sea-chaos. As in Psalm 29:3, the Warrior is about to battle Yam ("Sea"; cf. Job 7:12; 9:8). As in Isaiah 51:9, he will directly take on Rahab ("Surging One"; cf. Job 9:13; 26:12; Ps. 89:10). The encounter will be of great apocalyptic moment.

Before embarking on the Sea of Galilee, Jesus interacts with two would-be followers. In both cases, he forestalls their induction by stressing the arduousness and urgency of his itinerant work. Of special interest is Jesus's reference to himself in verse 20 as "the Son of Man." In the context of verse 20, the language expresses Jesus's full identification with the human condition (see Num. 23:19; Ps. 8:4; Ezek. 2:1). Prospective disciples must weigh the cost of siding with true human frailty and humility. As the passage proceeds, however, the idiom's second valence is increasingly relevant. The phrase also points to the glorious, end-time figure of might in Daniel 7:13–14 (cf. 1 Enoch 37–71). Rabbinic sources, following Daniel 7, know the idiom in this latter sense of an eschatological savior

(b. Sanh. 98a; y. Ta'an. 2.1; for Jesus as the apocalyptic "Son of Man," see Matt. 16:27–28; 24:30–31; 26:64; John 5:27).[13]

In Matthew 8:23, Jesus and the disciples board their boat and begin to cross the water. While Jesus sleeps, a great windstorm engulfs the craft. Waves crash aboard, certain to inundate and swamp it. The Greek term for "windstorm," *seismos*, is fraught with nuance, suggesting apocalyptic shaking and chaos (see Matt. 24:7; Rev. 6:12; and Ezek. 38:19 [in the Septuagint]).

As of verse 26, Jesus is awake but completely calm. Proving himself a brave heart, he reprimands the disciples' cowardice, rebukes the tempest, and creates a dead calm. The language of rebuking the sea storm is again provocative. Readers imagine the storm as a demon, a partisan of Rahab (Job 9:13) who has overstepped its bounds. This explains the disciples' reaction: "What sort of man is this?" The answer to their astonished question can only be that this must be the Divine Warrior incarnate. God alone defeats the chaos dragon.

Matthew 20:17–28
The Paradoxical Connection of Power and Suffering

Twice prior to Matthew 20, Jesus predicts his death in this Gospel (16:21–28; 17:22–23). This third revelation, however, gives specifics. Through a vicious alliance of Jerusalem's religious leaders and the imperial Roman authorities, Jesus will end up being mocked, flogged, and crucified. In the end, though, he will rise from the dead. As the passage proceeds, readers learn that Jesus's descent to death and rising to new life forms an extreme, paradigmatic witness to a mystery: selfless, sacrificial servanthood leads to victory and authority.

In verses 20–22 the passage directly addresses the tension between Jesus's royal prerogative and his destiny to suffer. Oblivious to Jesus's announcement of impending suffering, two of his disciples and their mother petition for prime positions in the messianic kingdom. They appear unable to grasp that Jesus's messiahship is necessarily catastrophic, entailing drinking God's cup of wrath (v. 22). Jesus reminds the petitioners that, in his reign, authority and greatness have nothing to do with ambition, eminence, and domination. Greatness in Jesus's brand of messianism derives paradoxically from sacrificial servanthood.

In discussing Isaiah's Servant Songs, above, we observed the tremendous power of purposeful vulnerability and sacrificial self-constriction. Verse 28 of our passage aptly cross-references Isaiah 53:11 and its image of the Servant offering his life for "many." Such servanthood heaps shame on the proud and violent, awakening them to their inhumanity. It also retracts one's own ego, freeing up space for encounters and intimate interactions with God's sublimity. Buoyed up by the experience of the wondrous, we selflessly, gratuitously uphold other persons, even enemies, nurturing human mutuality. As mutuality among persons builds, human interactions find harmony. Synergism mounts in a great expansion of spirit.

John 18:33–38a
Pilate and Jesus Discuss Authority and Truth

The dialogue between Pilate, the Roman governor, and Jesus in John 18:33–38a forms one key link in a chain of events leading from Jesus's arrest to his death by crucifixion. The death sentence sought by the religious authorities apparently required a Roman "trial" presided over by Pilate (John 18:28–19:16). Having received Jesus from the crowd, Pilate summons him inside the palace for a dialogue on the nature of his "kingdom." His query "Are you the King of the Jews?" (v. 33) raises *the* crucial question. Was Jesus a threat to Rome?

Jesus's response to Pilate, though evasive and enigmatic, is, in the end, negative. Despite a popular wish that he should reign as king in place of Rome, that is *not* his goal (see John 6:15). Jesus has broken no Roman law and is not a conventional threat to Rome. Readers can acknowledge this force of Jesus's response, however, without being very clear about Jesus's kingdom. A commonplace misunderstanding is that, for Jesus, the coming reign of God is purely spiritual—heavenly, and not involving any sort of terrestrial transformation.

In point of fact, Jesus's contrast of his reign and "this world" in John 18:36 does not entail any dualism between the spiritual and the terrestrial. The Greek term for "world" here, *kosmos*, in John's Gospel refers not to physical existence but to that which is hostile to God, lost in sin (see John 15:19; 17:15–16; cf. 1 John 4:5–6). Thus, what Jesus is saying is that his reign, authorized and originating "from above" (John 3:3), is of a completely different order than that in which Rome vies with other political forces for domination. Among modern translations, the *Complete Jewish Bible* does the best job with the claim in 18:36: "My kingship does not derive its authority from this world's order of things. . . . My kingship does not come from here."[14]

Jesus's reign is thus not ethereal but is rather a genuine rule expressed physically on earth. Jesus may be thinking of the nature of God's reign in Daniel (Dan. 2:44; 7:14, 27), where the apocalyptic kingdom of God is so qualitatively more substantial than all earth's kingdoms that its presence on earth immediately overwhelms mundane governments. Or again, recall how in Micah 5:2–4 a new sort of rule arising from Bethlehem, reliant on God's strength and centered in God's majesty, annuls and replaces Jerusalemite monarchic tyranny.

1 Corinthians 1:18–31
Christ Crucified as the Power of God

Near the beginning of his letter to the church at Corinth, the apostle Paul directs his readers toward the cross, the instrument of Christ's crucifixion. Verse 18 raises the question of the nature of the cross, which is perceived very differently by those who are followers of Jesus and by those who are not. This difference in perceptions relates, Paul argues, to a great paradox. In the case of Christ crucified, what seems foolish and weak actually constitutes absolute strength. Christ became weak in a show of "force" that makes humans strong. The shocking power of an ignominious death is so unconventional, in fact, that it overturns the ideas of all earth's experts. Earth's thinking about power and authority has been fully off.

The frailty and weakness of Christ, manifest in the cross, shames the strong (v. 27), thrusts aside all human boasting (v. 29). Such shaming is not incidental, for in the cross God deliberately humbles human pretension and hubris (v. 19, citing Isa. 29:14). So-called religious experts should take on the humility of Jeremiah, whom verse 31 cites. "Let the one who boasts, boast in the LORD" (see Jer. 9:24). All this theology of the cross has immediate relevance for Corinth, which was torn between rival teachers. If Paul's thinking about the cross is true, such conflicts of loyalty and communal divisions are fully undercut. All pretentious jockeying for status is shamed and humbled through the cross's "foolishness."

Galatians 5:22–26
The Generative Power of God's Spirit

In this section of his letter to the Galatians, the apostle Paul addresses the generative power of God's Holy Spirit. The presence of the Spirit in people's lives is a mark of the new age inaugurated by Christ's incarnation and resurrection. This age was anticipated in the Hebrew Scriptures in texts such as Isaiah 48:16b, which describes the Lord GOD sending both the Servant and the Spirit to accomplish redemption. Paul declares this new powerful age of redemption now manifest in the ethical renewal of believers. As natural as fruit on a fruit tree, the Spirit-directed life manifests powerful virtues and creates loving, joyful community.

Believers' renewal through the Spirit, Paul asserts, is itself a sharing in the death and resurrection of Jesus. As we share in Jesus's crucifixion, we "have crucified the flesh with its passions and desires" (v. 24). As with Jesus's language of "this world" in John 18:36, Paul's language of "the flesh" is no dualistic denigration of human embodiment (see, e.g., Gal. 3:3; Rom. 8:5–8). Rather, language of "the flesh" points at life lived in unruly autonomy, directed by "selfish and sinful cravings" (5:16).[15] To be baptized—sacramentally crucified—is to die to a self-oriented insistence on autonomy and to align with a powerful, selfless way of being human, a new, other-centered form of life. Believers owe this new life to the Spirit.

Philippians 2:5–11
Kenosis Leading to Exaltation

The celebrated "Kenosis Hymn" in Philippians 2 occurs in a section of the letter exhorting the church at Philippi to unity and humility. Scholars widely consider the hymn an early Christian song about Jesus, which Paul inserts into his letter as a breathtaking poetic evocation of reverence. The hymn has two stanzas, the first of which (vv. 7–8) depicts Christ's decent into humility and death, and the second of which (vv. 9–11) describes his resurrection and exaltation. Embracing servanthood, Christ paradoxically receives majesty.

What Christ could have clung to—equality with God—does eventually become his, for the very reason that he refused to cling to it (v. 9)! How is this conceivable? The meaning of verse 6 may be that *because of* his nature as God, Christ emptied himself (*kenosis*), embracing servanthood. The word "though" in the NRSV is actually not in the Greek text; the NIV is accurate to read: "Who, being in very nature God, did not consider equality with God something to be used to his own advantage."[16] Christian theological reflection on this passage might suggest that Christ's *kenosis* exemplifies the great synergistic power of the persons of the Trinity. That power derives from the persons' utter self-giving of themselves to each other. For the Philippians to imitate Christ in his other-centered humility and self-sacrifice is for them to join in the Trinity's synergism of mutual empowerment.

Revelation 12:7–12

Power Dynamics in Heaven and within the Terrestrial Plane

The scene that transpires in Revelation 12:7–12 is among the most fascinating and informative sequences in the book of Revelation. As in several of the passages considered above, the text recapitulates the ancient "combat myth," the victory of the Divine Warrior over the dragon. As in the other texts we have examined, mythology is critically appropriated here. Key modifications and spin-doctoring communicate a powerful theological message.

Strikingly, the passage's action occurs on two parallel ontological planes. On the upper plane, Michael leads a celestial army against the chaos dragon and his minions, defeating and banishing them (Rev. 12:7–9). On the lower, terrestrial plane, verses 10–11 describe heaven's victory over the dragon not in terms of violent field-combat but in terms of other-centered self-sacrifice. Christ (the "Lamb") along with his brave witnesses conquer the dragon "by the blood of the Lamb," refusing to "cling to life even in the face of death."

By the end of the passage, readers familiar with apocalyptic thought realize that a startling reversal of the genre's normal patterns has taken place. Usually in apocalyptic literature, paradigmatic events in heaven evoke parallel happenings on earth. Here, however, power dynamics in heaven shift in consequence of Christ's self-sacrifice on earth. An earthly, inner-historical event—the Lamb's sacrificial death—evokes an ontological transformation at the cosmic level. The effect is to overturn conventional thinking and highlight the huge power of one man's largely unnoticed act of selfless, self-giving love. Embracing frailty and willingly stepping into harm's way, the Lamb and his blood effect an ontological shift.

Notes

1. "Angelic beings" is as rendered in the New Revised Standard Version. For this rendition of the term "divine beings," see NJPS: New Jewish Publication Society Tanakh Translation (1985); also CEB: Common English Bible (2011).

2. For the location of these sites, see https://goo.gl/gYYyjh.

3. Kevin Madigan and Jon Douglas Levenson, *Resurrection: The Power of God for Christians and Jews* (New Haven, CT: Yale University Press, 2008), 193–96.

4. Stephen L. Cook, *Conversations with Scripture: 2 Isaiah* (Harrisburg, PA: Morehouse, 2008).

5. In this paragraph, all Bible verses are according to the translation *The Voice Bible: Step into the Story of Scripture* (Nashville: Thomas Nelson, 2012).

6. Translation: NRSV.

7. In this paragraph, Bible passages are according to the New Living Translation (Tyndale House Foundation, 1996).

8. For an accessible introduction to the Servant Songs and their meaning, see Cook, *Conversations with Scripture*.

9. See Brevard S. Childs, *Isaiah: A Commentary*, Old Testament Library (Louisville, KY: Westminster John Knox Press, 2001), 379, 383–84.

10. Translation: *New Jerusalem Bible*.

11. See Benjamin D. Sommer, *A Prophet Reads Scripture: Allusion in Isaiah 40–66*, Contraversions: Jews and Other Differences (Stanford, CA: Stanford University Press, 1998), 246–47.

12. See the excellent treatment of the notions of *sabr* (patience, forbearance) and martyrdom in Asma Afsaruddin, *Striving in the Path of God: Jihād and Martyrdom in Islamic Thought* (Oxford: Oxford University Press, 2013).

13. Aaron M. Gale, "Annotations to Matthew," in *The Jewish Annotated New Testament*, ed. Amy-Jill Levine and Marc Zvi Brettler (New York: Oxford University Press, 2011), 637.

14. David H. Stern, trans., *The Complete Jewish Bible: An English Version of the Tanakh (Old Testament) and B'rit Hadashah (New Testament)* (Clarksville, MD: Lederer Foundation, 1998).

15. Translation: *Voice Bible*.

16. See also *New Jerusalem Bible*.

The Bible on Divine and Human Power

Christian Texts for Dialogue

Old Testament

Psalm 29:1–11

The Divine Warrior as sovereign over both chaos and nature, the roots of apocalyptic notions of God's reign, and the resurrection of the dead

[1]Ascribe to the LORD, O heavenly beings,
      ascribe to the LORD glory and strength.
[2]Ascribe to the LORD the glory of his name;
      worship the LORD in holy splendor.
[3]The voice of the LORD is over the waters;
      the God of glory thunders,
      the LORD, over mighty waters.
[4]The voice of the LORD is powerful;
      the voice of the LORD is full of majesty.
[5]The voice of the LORD breaks the cedars;
      the LORD breaks the cedars of Lebanon.
[6]He makes Lebanon skip like a calf,
      and Sirion like a young wild ox.
[7]The voice of the LORD flashes forth flames of fire.
[8]The voice of the LORD shakes the wilderness;
      the LORD shakes the wilderness of Kadesh.
[9]The voice of the LORD causes the oaks to whirl,
      and strips the forest bare;
      and in his temple all say, "Glory!"
[10]The LORD sits enthroned over the flood;
      the LORD sits enthroned as king forever.

[11]May the LORD give strength to his people!
May the LORD bless his people with peace!

Isaiah 55:6–11

God's towering transcendence and irresistible Word

[6]Seek the LORD while he may be found,
call upon him while he is near;
[7]let the wicked forsake their way,
and the unrighteous their thoughts;
let them return to the LORD, that he may have mercy on them,
and to our God, for he will abundantly pardon.
[8]For my thoughts are not your thoughts,
nor are your ways my ways, says the LORD.
[9]For as the heavens are higher than the earth,
so are my ways higher than your ways
and my thoughts than your thoughts.
[10]For as the rain and the snow come down from heaven,
and do not return there until they have watered the earth,
making it bring forth and sprout,
giving seed to the sower and bread to the eater,
[11]so shall my word be that goes out from my mouth;
it shall not return to me empty,
but it shall accomplish that which I purpose,
and succeed in the thing for which I sent it.

Isaiah 51:9–16

God's Power attested in cosmogony, exodus, and the liberation from Babylonian exile

[9]Awake, awake, put on strength,
O arm of the LORD!
Awake, as in days of old, the generations of long ago!
Was it not you who cut Rahab in pieces, who pierced the dragon?
[10]Was it not you who dried up the sea,
the waters of the great deep;
who made the depths of the sea a way
for the redeemed to cross over?
[11]So the ransomed of the LORD shall return,
and come to Zion with singing;

everlasting joy shall be upon their heads;
>they shall obtain joy and gladness,
>and sorrow and sighing shall flee away.

[12]I, I am he who comforts you;
>why then are you afraid of a mere mortal who must die,
>a human being who fades like grass?

[13]You have forgotten the LORD, your Maker,
>who stretched out the heavens
>and laid the foundations of the earth.

You fear continually all day long
>because of the fury of the oppressor,

who is bent on destruction.
>But where is the fury of the oppressor?

[14]The oppressed shall speedily be released;
>they shall not die and go down to the Pit,
>nor shall they lack bread.

[15]For I am the LORD your God,
>who stirs up the sea so that its waves roar—
>the LORD of hosts is his name.

[16]I have put my words in your mouth,
>and hidden you in the shadow of my hand,

stretching out the heavens
>and laying the foundations of the earth,
>and saying to Zion, "You are my people."

Isaiah 31:1–3

God's "Cosmic Prerogative," which relativizes all human powers and alliances

[1]Alas for those who go down to Egypt for help
>and who rely on horses,

who trust in chariots because they are many
>and in horsemen because they are very strong,

but do not look to the Holy One of Israel
>or consult the LORD!

[2]Yet he too is wise and brings disaster;
>he does not call back his words,

but will rise against the house of the evildoers,
>and against the helpers of those who work iniquity.

[3]The Egyptians are human, and not God;
>their horses are flesh, and not spirit.

When the LORD stretches out his hand,
    the helper will stumble, and the one helped will fall,
    and they will all perish together.

Exodus 14:10–15:3

God's classic mighty work at the Red Sea

[10]As Pharaoh drew near, the Israelites looked back, and there were the Egyptians advancing on them. In great fear the Israelites cried out to the LORD. [11]They said to Moses, "Was it because there were no graves in Egypt that you have taken us away to die in the wilderness? What have you done to us, bringing us out of Egypt? [12]Is this not the very thing we told you in Egypt, 'Let us alone and let us serve the Egyptians'? For it would have been better for us to serve the Egyptians than to die in the wilderness." [13]But Moses said to the people, "Do not be afraid, stand firm, and see the deliverance that the LORD will accomplish for you today; for the Egyptians whom you see today you shall never see again. [14]The LORD will fight for you, and you have only to keep still." [15]Then the LORD said to Moses, "Why do you cry out to me? Tell the Israelites to go forward. [16]But you lift up your staff, and stretch out your hand over the sea and divide it, that the Israelites may go into the sea on dry ground. [17]Then I will harden the hearts of the Egyptians so that they will go in after them; and so I will gain glory for myself over Pharaoh and all his army, his chariots, and his chariot drivers."

[18]And the Egyptians shall know that I am the LORD, when I have gained glory for myself over Pharaoh, his chariots, and his chariot drivers." [19]The angel of God who was going before the Israelite army moved and went behind them; and the pillar of cloud moved from in front of them and took its place behind them. [20]It came between the army of Egypt and the army of Israel. And so the cloud was there with the darkness, and it lit up the night; one did not come near the other all night. [21]Then Moses stretched out his hand over the sea. The LORD drove the sea back by a strong east wind all night, and turned the sea into dry land; and the waters were divided. [22]The Israelites went into the sea on dry ground, the waters forming a wall for them on their right and on their left. [23]The Egyptians pursued, and went into the sea after them, all of Pharaoh's horses, chariots, and chariot drivers. [24]At the morning watch the LORD in the pillar of fire and cloud looked down upon the Egyptian army, and threw the Egyptian army into panic. [25]He clogged their chariot wheels so that they turned with difficulty. The Egyptians said, "Let us flee from the Israelites, for the LORD is fighting for them against Egypt." [26]Then the LORD said to Moses, "Stretch out your hand over the sea, so that the water may come back upon the Egyptians, upon their chariots and chariot drivers." [27]So Moses stretched out his hand over the sea, and at dawn the sea returned to its normal depth. As the Egyptians fled before it, the LORD tossed the

Egyptians into the sea. [28]The waters returned and covered the chariots and the chariot drivers, the entire army of Pharaoh that had followed them into the sea; not one of them remained.

[29]But the Israelites walked on dry ground through the sea, the waters forming a wall for them on their right and on their left. [30]Thus the LORD saved Israel that day from the Egyptians; and Israel saw the Egyptians dead on the seashore. [31]Israel saw the great work that the LORD did against the Egyptians. So the people feared the LORD and believed in the LORD and in his servant Moses.

15 [1]Then Moses and the Israelites sang this song to the LORD:

"I will sing to the LORD, for he has triumphed gloriously;
    horse and rider he has thrown into the sea.
[2]The LORD is my strength and my might,
    and he has become my salvation;
this is my God, and I will praise him,
    my father's God, and I will exalt him.
[3]The LORD is a warrior;
    the LORD is his name."

Isaiah 52:13–53:3

God's power—the "arm of the Lord"—revealed paradoxically in lowliness and suffering

[13]See, my servant shall prosper;
    he shall be exalted and lifted up,
    and shall be very high.
[14]Just as there were many who were astonished at him
    —so marred was his appearance,
        beyond human semblance,
    and his form beyond that of mortals—
[15]so he shall startle many nations;
    kings shall shut their mouths because of him;
for that which had not been told them they shall see,
    and that which they had not heard they shall contemplate.
53 [1]Who has believed what we have heard?
    And to whom has the arm of the LORD been revealed?
[2]For he grew up before him like a young plant,
    and like a root out of dry ground;
he had no form or majesty that we should look at him,
    nothing in his appearance that we should desire him.

[3]He was despised and rejected by others;
>   a man of suffering and acquainted with infirmity;
and as one from whom others hide their faces
>   he was despised, and we held him of no account.

Hosea 11:1–9

God's power and vulnerability in conflict

[1]When Israel was a child, I loved him,
>   and out of Egypt I called my son.
[2]The more I called them,
>   the more they went from me;
they kept sacrificing to the Baals,
>   and offering incense to idols.
[3]Yet it was I who taught Ephraim to walk,
>   I took them up in my arms;
>   but they did not know that I healed them.
[4]I led them with cords of human kindness,
>   with bands of love.
I was to them like those
>   who lift infants to their cheeks.
>   I bent down to them and fed them.
[5]They shall return to the land of Egypt,
>   and Assyria shall be their king,
>   because they have refused to return to me.
[6]The sword rages in their cities,
>   it consumes their oracle-priests,
>   and devours because of their schemes.
[7]My people are bent on turning away from me.
>   To the Most High they call,
>   but he does not raise them up at all.
[8]How can I give you up, Ephraim?
>   How can I hand you over, O Israel?
How can I make you like Admah?
>   How can I treat you like Zeboiim?
My heart recoils within me;
>   my compassion grows warm and tender.
[9]I will not execute my fierce anger;
>   I will not again destroy Ephraim;
for I am God and no mortal,
>   the Holy One in your midst,
>   and I will not come in wrath.

New Testament

Matthew 8:14-17

Jesus's divine power and prerogative over disease and demons; quotation of a suffering messiah motif from Isaiah 53:4.

[14]When Jesus entered Peter's house, he saw his mother-in-law lying in bed with a fever; [15]he touched her hand, and the fever left her, and she got up and began to serve him. [16]That evening they brought to him many who were possessed with demons; and he cast out the spirits with a word, and cured all who were sick. [17]This was to fulfill what had been spoken through the prophet Isaiah, "He took our infirmities and bore our diseases."

Matthew 8:18-27

Jesus's cosmic and apocalyptic power over chaos; verse 20 contains the "Son of Man" eschatological-messiah motif from Daniel 7:13–14; the idiom can also express frailty and humility, and does so here.

[18]Now when Jesus saw great crowds around him, he gave orders to go over to the other side. [19]A scribe then approached and said, "Teacher, I will follow you wherever you go." [20]And Jesus said to him, "Foxes have holes, and birds of the air have nests; but the Son of Man has nowhere to lay his head." [21]Another of his disciples said to him, "Lord, first let me go and bury my father." [22]But Jesus said to him, "Follow me, and let the dead bury their own dead."

[23]And when he got into the boat, his disciples followed him. [24]A windstorm arose on the sea, so great that the boat was being swamped by the waves; but he was asleep. [25]And they went and woke him up, saying, "Lord, save us! We are perishing!" [26]And he said to them, "Why are you afraid, you of little faith?" Then he got up and rebuked the winds and the sea; and there was a dead calm. [27]They were amazed, saying, "What sort of man is this, that even the winds and the sea obey him?"

Matthew 20:17-28

The text shows well the paradoxical connection of power and suffering/ death, of servanthood and greatness (v. 26); verse 28 echoes Isaiah 53:11.

[17]While Jesus was going up to Jerusalem, he took the twelve disciples aside by themselves, and said to them on the way, [18]"See, we are going up to Jerusalem, and the Son of Man will be handed over to the chief priests and scribes, and they

will condemn him to death; [19]then they will hand him over to the Gentiles to be mocked and flogged and crucified; and on the third day he will be raised."

[20]Then the mother of the sons of Zebedee came to him with her sons, and kneeling before him, she asked a favor of him. [21]And he said to her, "What do you want?" She said to him, "Declare that these two sons of mine will sit, one at your right hand and one at your left, in your kingdom." [22]But Jesus answered, "You do not know what you are asking. Are you able to drink the cup that I am about to drink?" They said to him, "We are able." [23]He said to them, "You will indeed drink my cup, but to sit at my right hand and at my left, this is not mine to grant, but it is for those for whom it has been prepared by my Father."

[24]When the ten heard it, they were angry with the two brothers. [25]But Jesus called them to him and said, "You know that the rulers of the Gentiles lord it over them, and their great ones are tyrants over them. [26]It will not be so among you; but whoever wishes to be great among you must be your servant, [27]and whoever wishes to be first among you must be your slave; [28]just as the Son of Man came not to be served but to serve, and to give his life a ransom for many."

John 18:33–38a

Pilate and Jesus discussing authority and truth.

[33]Then Pilate entered the headquarters again, summoned Jesus, and asked him, "Are you the King of the Jews?" [34]Jesus answered, "Do you ask this on your own, or did others tell you about me?" [35]Pilate replied, "I am not a Jew, am I? Your own nation and the chief priests have handed you over to me. What have you done?" [36]Jesus answered, "My kingdom is not from this world. If my kingdom were from this world, my followers would be fighting to keep me from being handed over to the Jews. But as it is, my kingdom is not from here." [37]Pilate asked him, "So you are a king?" Jesus answered, "You say that I am a king. For this I was born, and for this I came into the world, to testify to the truth. Everyone who belongs to the truth listens to my voice." [38]Pilate asked him, "What is truth?"

1 Corinthians 1:18–31

Christ crucified as the power of God.

[18]For the message about the cross is foolishness to those who are perishing, but to us who are being saved it is the power of God. [19]For it is written,

"I will destroy the wisdom of the wise,
    and the discernment of the discerning I will thwart."

[20]Where is the one who is wise? Where is the scribe? Where is the debater of this age? Has not God made foolish the wisdom of the world? [21]For since, in the

wisdom of God, the world did not know God through wisdom, God decided, through the foolishness of our proclamation, to save those who believe. [22]For Jews demand signs and Greeks desire wisdom, [23]but we proclaim Christ crucified, a stumbling block to Jews and foolishness to Gentiles, [24]but to those who are the called, both Jews and Greeks, Christ the power of God and the wisdom of God. [25]For God's foolishness is wiser than human wisdom, and God's weakness is stronger than human strength.

[26]Consider your own call, brothers and sisters: not many of you were wise by human standards, not many were powerful, not many were of noble birth. [27]But God chose what is foolish in the world to shame the wise; God chose what is weak in the world to shame the strong; [28]God chose what is low and despised in the world, things that are not, to reduce to nothing things that are, [29]so that no one might boast in the presence of God. [30]He is the source of your life in Christ Jesus, who became for us wisdom from God, and righteousness and sanctification and redemption, [31]in order that, as it is written, "Let the one who boasts, boast in the Lord."

Galatians 5:22–26

The generative power of God's Spirit is manifested in the ethical renewal of believers, itself a sharing in the death and resurrection of Jesus.

[22]By contrast, the fruit of the Spirit is love, joy, peace, patience, kindness, generosity, faithfulness, [23]gentleness, and self-control. There is no law against such things. [24]And those who belong to Christ Jesus have crucified the flesh with its passions and desires. [25]If we live by the Spirit, let us also be guided by the Spirit. [26]Let us not become conceited, competing against one another, envying one another.

Philippians 2:5–11

Kenosis leading to exaltation

[5]Let the same mind be in you that was in Christ Jesus,
  [6]who, though he was in the form of God,
  did not regard equality with God as something to be exploited,
[7]but emptied himself,
  taking the form of a slave,
  being born in human likeness.
And being found in human form,
  [8]he humbled himself
  and became obedient to the point of death—
  even death on a cross.

[9]Therefore God also highly exalted him
    and gave him the name
    that is above every name,
[10]so that at the name of Jesus
    every knee should bend,
    in heaven and on earth and under the earth,
[11]and every tongue should confess
    that Jesus Christ is Lord,
    to the glory of God the Father.

Revelation 12:7–12

Archangel Michael's heavenly field-combat victory parallels Christ's dying and rising on earth. Power dynamics in heaven shift in consequence of Christ's sacrifice within the terrestrial plane.

[7]And war broke out in heaven; Michael and his angels fought against the dragon. The dragon and his angels fought back, [8]but they were defeated, and there was no longer any place for them in heaven. [9]The great dragon was thrown down, that ancient serpent, who is called the Devil and Satan, the deceiver of the whole world—he was thrown down to the earth, and his angels were thrown down with him.

[10]Then I heard a loud voice in heaven, proclaiming,
"Now have come the salvation and the power
    and the kingdom of our God
    and the authority of his Messiah,
for the accuser of our comrades has been thrown down,
    who accuses them day and night before our God.
[11]But they have conquered him by the blood of the Lamb
    and by the word of their testimony,
for they did not cling to life even in the face of death.
[12]Rejoice then, you heavens
    and those who dwell in them!
But woe to the earth and the sea,
    for the devil has come down to you
with great wrath,
    because he knows that his time is short!"

Note

All Bible passages in this chapter are according to the New Revised Standard Version (NRSV).

PART THREE

The Theme of "Power and Community" in Islamic and Christian Writings

Ideals and Realities of Muslim Community Ordering

AHMET ALIBAŠIĆ

In addressing the question of the nature of humans and community who have recognized God's power, this essay follows the approach often used to introduce Muslim children to the normative system of Islam. Muslim children are told that in order to be good Muslims, they must properly maintain several relationships: with their Creator, with their fellow humans (Muslims and non-Muslims, especially parents, relatives, and neighbors), and ultimately with the rest of what God has created. In addition, they also have duties toward themselves. In effect, a power matrix of Muslim individual and community emerges.[1]

In relation to the Creator, as is commonly understood, a believer is expected to be an obedient servant, a slave even: "I created jinn and humankind only that they might worship Me. I seek no livelihood from them, nor do I ask that they should feed Me. Indeed, God is the Provider, the Possessor of Power, the Unbreakably Mighty," proclaims God in the Qur'an (51:56–58).[2] In another place He commands, "Obey God and obey His messenger. If you turn away, then the duty of Our messenger is only to convey the message plainly" (Q. 64:12). The most perfect of God's servants is the Prophet himself. That makes this potentially humiliating and demeaning idea and relationship emancipating and empowering as it translates into, I am not subordinate to anyone or anything else other than God! Elsewhere God is said to be self-sufficient (*al-ghaniyy*), while humans need Him (Q. 35:14). Man's troubles start when he imagines that he is independent from his Creator (Q. 96:6–7). However, like most other religious ideas, the idea of servitude to God can be and has been conceptualized in ways that constrain humans, including their rational capacities, and in such a way that makes them easy prey to superstition and to all forms of manipulation.[3]

Before moving on, it is worth noting that there are other readings of the same texts where worship (*'ibada*) is read to mean "to know God."[4] That reading obviously takes the Qur'anic text into a different direction. This diversity of readings is not unique to this verse. In our case, vicegerency of man on earth (*khilafa*) and the issue of friendship (*wilaya*) have also been interpreted in ways that would not leave us with much to discuss. According to some interpretations, when the Qur'an speaks about *khilafa*, it is simply referring to successive generations of humans, while *wilaya* is about inheritance and not about the high wall of separation between Muslims and non-Muslims.[5]

Back to the Muslim power matrix, in relation to nature, contemporary authors emphasize the concept of its subjugation (*taskhir*) to humans, who are God's representatives (*khulafa*) on earth.[6] Traditionally, however, Muslims were thinking of nature more in terms of its appreciation and preservation because of its presumed sanctity or because of self-interest.[7] In preindustrial societies, a tree cut meant less fruit and less shade on the road. Food thrown out meant less stuff to survive on, and so on.

The strong person is the one who controls himself or herself, especially when angry, not the one who has more muscles. True, a strong believer—in faith and otherwise—is better than the weak one, but both are fine: "A strong believer is better and is more lovable to Allah than a weak believer, and there is good in everyone."[8]

The Muslim community itself is hailed in the Qur'an, in passages such as Surat Āl 'Imran [3]:103, for its brotherhood, unity, and solidarity. In Surat al-Tawba, we read, "The believers, both men and women, are the protecting friends of one another; they enjoin the right and forbid what is wrong" (9:71). Similarly, in Surat al-Anfal, "the disbelievers are protectors of one another. If you do not do likewise, there will be confusion in the land and great corruption" (8:73). Indeed, the believers are like a single body, a hadith asserts: "The parable of the believers in their affection, mercy, and compassion for each other is that of a body. When any limb aches, the whole body reacts with sleeplessness and fever."[9]

However, ideals are not always realities. Therefore, the Qur'an addresses less pleasant but more realistic scenarios when the Muslim community fails to live up to those high expectations. Then an effort needs to be made to reconcile conflicting parties, but eventually even the use of force is authorized in order to bring aggressors to justice:

> If two parties of believers fall to fighting [each other], then try to make peace between them. And if one party does wrong to the other, fight the wrongdoers until they submit to God's command; then, if they return, make peace between them justly, and act equitably. Indeed, God loves the equitable. The believers are nothing but brothers. Therefore, make peace between your brethren and be mindful of your duty to God, so that perhaps you may receive mercy. (Q. 49:9–10)[10]

Contrary to common practice among warring parties, the Qur'an here uses no harsh language when describing such occasions. After all, the believers are brothers, and every effort should be made to reconcile among them. To help the reconciliation, different rules of warfare apply (e.g., no booty, no prisoners). Furthermore, many jurists will not require the wrong party to repair the damage it has done.[11] Still, according to Al-Tabari (d. 923), not confronting troublemakers is not an option, as it would encourage sinners and hypocrites:

> If in every discord between two factions, one has the duty to flee, stay at home, and withhold one's sword, then no single law would ever be upheld and no injustice would ever be negated. Moreover, every hypocrite and transgressor would find a way to unlawfully seize what Allah made unlawful from the wealth of the people, their women and spilling their blood, by joining forces with one another, while the Muslims would withdraw their hands by claiming this is a discord that they have been prohibited from getting involved in and have been ordered to flee, which is in contradiction to the Prophetic teaching "Seize the hands of the foolish ones" (i.e. stop them).[12]

What is potentially interesting to us here is that God is delegating the job of righting the wrong party to Muslims themselves. Similarly, the Qur'an emphasizes the role and importance of human agency in God's plans regarding the maintenance of global order when stating that "had it not been for God's repelling some people by means of others, many cloisters and churches and synagogues and mosques, wherein the name of God is often mentioned, would assuredly have been destroyed" (Q. 22:40). In his commentary on this verse, Al-Qurtubi notes various interpretations, but all of them include humans stopping other humans from getting away with their bad deeds.[13]

What makes Muslim Ummah truly exceptional and the best of all communities, says the Qur'an, is its commitment to godliness: "You are the best community that has been raised up for humankind. You enjoin right conduct and forbid the wrong; and you believe in God" (Q. 3:110). To al-Qurtubi, this is a distinguishing feature between true believers and hypocrites.[14] No amount of passive individual piety can compensate for the failure to carry out this duty. (By way of illustration, the Prophet reportedly told his companions about the Angel Jibril, who once was sent by God to destroy a town. Jibril asked if the pious man in the town, who spent his every moment in the remembrance of God, was also meant to be destroyed. God told him to annihilate that "pious" man first since he did not bother to guide his people.[15]) This is probably so because, to be true seekers of good, Muslims first have to be committed to it in their own individual and communal lives. They have to be just, even against themselves and their parents and relatives: "O you who believe! Be staunch in justice, witnesses for God, even though it be against yourselves or your parents or your kindred. Whether the case be of a rich person or a poor person, God is nearer to both than you are). . . . Those who choose disbelievers for their allies instead of believers: do they seek power at their hands? Indeed, all power belongs to God" (Q. 4:135, 139).

Individually and collectively, Muslims are expected to be independent-minded and swim against the tide if need be, for Prophet Muhammad, peace be upon him, reportedly commanded Muslims: "Do not be blind followers. Do not say: if people do good I will join them in doing good and if they do bad we join them, but be of principle. When people do good you do good as well but when people do wrong you should not join them."[16] Furthermore, there is no obedience to humankind in disobedience to Allah; obedience is due in good (*ma'ruf*) things.[17]

The Qur'an does not shy away from the use of power. It allows for reciprocity but encourages forgiveness repeatedly:

> And what God has is better and more lasting for those who believe and put their trust in the Lord, and those who shun the worst of sins and indecencies and—when they are angry—forgive, and those who answer the call of their Lord and perform prayer, and whose affairs are a matter of counsel, and who spend of what We have bestowed on them, and those who—when great wrong is done to them—defend themselves. The recompence of an ill-deed is an ill similar to it. But whosoever pardons and makes amends, his wage is the affair of God. Indeed, He loves not wrong-doers. And whoever defends himself after he has suffered wrong—for such, there is no way (of blame) against them. The way (of blame) is only against those who oppress humankind, and wrongfully rebel in the earth. For such there is a painful doom. And whoever is patient and forgives—that, indeed, is (of) the steadfast heart of things. (Q. 42:36b–43)

The short reference to the manner in which the Muslim community manages its common affairs is of systemic importance as it gives a different perspective on the issue of consultation (*shura*), which is usually understood as the non-obliging consultation of rulers with their subjects. Here there are no rulers and subjects, only equal members of the community.[18] It is probably this presupposition of equality that makes this principle so unacceptable to some Muslims: they simply cannot accept the idea that all Muslims are equal.

In line with the idea of social contract between the ruler and the society, Abu Bakr, in his inaugural speech, proclaimed,

> I've been appointed as ruler over you, though I'm not the best of you. If I do well (to you) then you should support me, and if I do evil (to you) then you should guide me to what is right. . . . You should obey me as long as I comply with (the orders and instructions of) God and His Messenger. But, if I deviate (from that), then you should have the right not to obey me.[19]

This, of course, does not resolve all the problems between people and their government but at least makes clear that rulers are subject to a higher will, a constitution of a kind. Later Islamic tradition, both textual and interpretative, is very ambivalent, to say the least, when it comes to the obligation of the community to obey the ruler, whatever his acts. Al-Nawawi (d. 1277), in his commentary on *Sahih Muslim*, writes that the vast majority of Sunni scholars agree that a ruler should not be removed or rebelled against because of his sins, injustice, or denial of rights. Even worse, Abu Bakr ibn Mujahid (d. 936) claimed (at least later) consensus on this. It could be observed that where one discursively stands on this issue depends on where one stands in power structures.

Still, that being said, there are no blank guarantees to Muslims. If they fail in performing their duties, God will replace them:

> O you who believe! If any of you becomes a renegade from his religion, (know that in [your] stead) God will bring a people whom He loves and who love Him, humble toward believers, stern toward disbelievers, striving in the way of God, and fearing not the blame of any blamer. Such is the grace of God which He gives to whomever He will. God is All-Embracing, All-Knowing. Your guardian can be only God; and His messenger and those who believe, who perform prayer and pay the alms tax, and bow down (in worship). And whosoever takes God and His messenger and those who believe for protection (will know that), indeed: the party of God, they are the victorious. (Q. 5:54–56)

So, the top spot among communities must constantly be deserved. And those who deserve it will triumph. But in what way? The answer comes in another verse: "Indeed, We have written in the Psalms, after the Reminder: 'My righteous servants will inherit the earth'" (Q. 21:105). Contrary to what could be understood when reading this verse in isolation, God seems to be promising Muslims the land of Paradise. This is the prevailing understanding among early commentators, including Ibn Abbas, Sa'id ibn Jubayr, and Mujahid as well as Al-Tabari's preferred interpretation.

The next question, then, is, Which is the way to Paradise? How do we get there? Ayatullah Ruhullah Khumayni, the leader of the Iranian revolution, argue that an Islamic government headed by an Islamic scholar would do the trick. It is enemies of Islam who claim that Islam "only concerns itself with the rules of menstruation and childbirth" and not with ordering of life or society or creating a government. In reality, Khumayni asserts, Islam is meant to last forever; therefore, such a government must exist. Otherwise, "social chaos, corruption and ideological and moral deviation would prevail. This can be prevented only through the creation of a just government that runs all aspects of life." That just government will be established by a knowledgeable and just jurisprudent who will run the social affairs that Prophet Muhammad, peace be upon him, and Imam Ali used to run in accordance with the Shari'a, and it is the duty of the people to obey him.[20]

On the contrary, Abdullahi Ahmed An-Na'im proposes that a secular state—i.e., religiously neutral state—is a precondition for being a Muslim by conviction, "simply because compliance with Shari'a cannot be coerced by fear of state institutions or faked to appease officials." He asserts that he is promoting genuine religiosity by his call for the secular state because in such a state Shari'a shapes the value system of citizens who then through democratic process influence public policies.[21]

In between these two radical options are two other proposals that envision a scheme in which, in addition to individual actors and government, society and community are empowered to play a significant role in carrying out collective religious duties expected of Muslims. Khaled Abou El Fadl, for one, finds the secularist position to be as problematic as the one promoted by "religious puritans," for the secular state is not value neutral:

> If religion is excluded from the public sphere, this only means that the shared space occupied by civic institutions favors nonreligious rationales, arguments, and values . . . , if as a condition of engaging the public sphere citizens are required to omit God from the public discourse, by definition, the state is favoring discourses that are godless.[22]

This would deny Muslims an opportunity to carry out the obligation to investigate what God wants from and for them individually and collectively. "The theological demand to bear witness on God's behalf and to enjoin the good and resist what is not good (*al-amr bi'l ma'ruf wa'l nahy 'an al-munkar*) is core to the imperative of furthering godly social norms. . . ('the imperative of godliness')."[23]

Abou El Fadl equally disapproves of calls for the state's wholesale enactment of Shari'a. The right thing to aim for is to have the state implement socially mediated Shari'a norms in social acts, not in acts of worship and rituals (*'ibadat*) or strict self-interest, that is, acts with no social ramifications because those are based on revelation. The Shari'a needs to play a role in regulating social acts because it is not neutral on social issues: "For one thing, the Qur'anic commandment to enjoin the good and resist the evil is addressed to the umma (Muslim nation) as a whole."[24] This is in addition to collective duties of establishing justice and conducting all public affairs by consultation. He eventually arrives at a daring conclusion:

> Democracy and human rights cannot be achieved without normative commitments at the individual and societal levels. It is the duty of Muslim intellectuals to do the cumbersome and toilsome task of persuading their co-religionists that a private and public commitment to democracy and human rights is also a commitment to shari'a, and also that in the contemporary world a commitment in favour of shari'a is best realised through a commitment to democracy and human rights.[25]

This is easier said than done, as Murad Hofmann must have learned.[26] He has written a clear, succinct summary of the characteristics of Islamic political system that, despite all his efforts, is an interpretative minefield both from the liberal democratic and orthodox Muslim points of view. Consider, for instance, the first feature: "All Muslims should live in a world-wide, but decentralized Islamic commonwealth organized as a republic."[27] A single Muslim polity is scary to many non-Muslims; it does not matter that it is a republic and that it is decentralized. On the other hand, most Muslims have adjusted to their nation-states. In addition, royalists hate the idea of republic. All other twelve points are equally or even more "controversial."

Louay Safi, a US scholar of Syrian background, has developed an argument for a bigger role of the community in the modern state by emphasizing the priority of the institutions of civil society over those of the state, which is necessary in order to limit the power of the modern state. Safi dedicates significant energy to distinguishing the political structures of the Ummah and the state and, consequently, the functions of the Shari'a and those of the state. When moral and educational functions of the Ummah are mixed with legal functions of the state, the idea of a totalitarian Islamic state inevitably emerges. There is no denial that "the main objective of establishing a political system is to create the general conditions that allow the people to realize their duties as moral agents of the Divine will (*khulafa'*), not to impose the teachings of Islam by force."[28]

Key to differentiating between the roles of the community and the state is the division of legislation into distinct areas that reflect the diversity of the polity with some legislative and judicial powers tied to the society directly. Through differential structure of the law the tendency of the modern state to centralize power is countered and guarantees are extended to religious minorities. This, Safi believes, could be a profound, significant contribution of the Islamic political thought toward "reclaiming the moral core of social life and preserving religious traditions, without sacrificing the principle of freedom and equality promoted by the modern state."[29] Historically, Muslim society managed to limit the actions of rulers by entrusting to civic institutions many of the functions of the contemporary secular state, including education, health, and legislation. The state was mainly concerned with security and defense and was "the last resort in questions relating to dispensation of justice."[30] After asserting the notions of individual freedom and equality as intrinsic to Islamic political thought, Safi goes on to conclude,

> By freeing civil society from the heavy hand of the state, and by extending individual liberties to the community and recognizing the moral autonomy of social groups, social and religious groups under the Islamic conception of law (Shari'a) would have the capacity to legislate their internal morality and affairs in their communities. While the new sphere of freedom acquired under this arrangement would allow for differentiation among citizens,

equality would have to be maintained as the criterion of justice in the new area of public law, and in access to public institutions—that is, in matters relating to shared interests and inter-communal relations.[31]

Muslims obviously struggle with the questions of power. What is less obvious is that the real challenge for Muslims today is not so much their attitude to power as much as it is their attitude to powerlessness, because, as Shabbir Akhtar says, "Traditionally, Muslims developed only a theology of power since Muhammad left an undiluted legacy of success."[32] However, today powerlessness and defeat are the order of the day in the Muslim world. All signs are indicating that its near future will be its extended present more than anything else.

Notes

1. The Muslim community's power relations with non-Muslims are discussed in this volume by Mahan Mirza.
2. Unless otherwise indicated, Qur'an verses are according to Mohammed Marmaduke Pickthall, *The Meaning of the Glorious Qur'ān* (London: Knopf, 1930), adapted slightly.
3. AbdulHamid Abu Sulayman, *Inhiyar al-hadara al-islamiyya wa i'ada binaiha: al-judhur al-thaqafiyya wa al-tarbawiyya* (Herndon, VA: International Institute of Islamic Thought, 2016), 59–60.
4. Al-Qurtubi (d. 1273) attributes this opinion to Mujahid (d. 722).
5. See Al-Tabari's commentary on verses Q. 2:30 and 8:73.
6. 'Abd al Majid al Najjar, *The Vicegerency of Man: Between Revelation and Reason* (Herndon, VA: International Institute of Islamic Thought, 2000). See Q. 2:30; Q. 45:13.
7. S. H. Nasr, *Man and Nature: The Spiritual Crisis of Modern Man* (London: Unwin, 1990).
8. *Sahih Muslim,* no. 2664.
9. *Sahih al-Bukhari,* no. 5665; and *Sahih Muslim,* no. 2586.
10. The third caliph, Uthman, sounds equally realistic when he states that God deters more people by state power than He does with the Qur'an: "Inna Allah yaza' bi al-sultan ma la yaza' bi al-Qur'an."
11. Cf. Al-Zamakhshari commentary on Q. 49:9. Muslim infighting is always disturbing and difficult to fathom, and especially so when the best generation is involved in it. Here is Al-Qurtubi's summary of what the right attitude toward infighting should be: "It is not permissible to attribute to any of the companion a certain error, for all of them did ijtihad in what they were doing (*kulluhum ijtahadu fi ma fa'aluh*) and all sought God by their deeds. All of them are our leaders and we worship God by not discussing that which happened amongst them."
12. From the comment on Q. 49:9 in *Tafsīr al-Qurtubi.* Translation taken from Great Muslim Quotes, "Muḥammad b. Jarīr Al-Ṭabarī [d. 310H/923CE]" (n.d.), http://greatmuslimquotes.com/category/name/mu%E1%B8%A5ammad-b-jarir-al-%E1%B9%ADabari-d-310h923ce/.

13. Muhammad b. Ahmad al-Qurtubi, *Al-Jami' li Ahkam al-Qur'an* (Beirut: Muassasa al-Risala, 2006), 14:408–12.

14. Here, too, we come across readings that limit this passage to the first generation of Muslims but that are neither its only nor dominant understanding.

15. Al-Tirmidhi, no. 5142.

16. Al-Tirmidhi, no. 2007. Most probably a saying of Ibn Mas'ud.

17. *La ta'a li makhluq fi ma'siya al-khaliq* (from *Musnad Ahmad*) or *la ta'a li bashar fi ma'siya Allah; innama al-ta'a fi al-ma'ruf.* Found in *Sahih al-Bukhari, Sahih Muslim,* and other hadith collections).

18. Fazlur Rahman, "The Principle of Shura and the Role of the Umma in Islam," in *State Politics and Islam,* ed. Mumtaz Ahmad (Indianapolis: American Trust Publications, 1986).

19. Khalid Muhammad Khalid, *Successors of the Messenger,* translated by Muhammad M. Al-Sharif (Beirut, Dar al-kotob al-ilmiyah, 2005), 91.

20. Ayatullah Ruhullah Khumayni, "Islamic Government [*Vilayat-i Faqih*]," in *Islam in Transition: Muslim Perspectives,* 2nd ed., ed. John Donohue and John Esposito, 332–40 (New York: Oxford University Press, 2007), 333, 334, and 338.

21. Abdullahi A. An-Na'im, *Islam and the Secular State: Negotiating the Future of Shari'a* (Cambridge, MA: Harvard University Press, 2008), 1.

22. Khaled Abou El Fadl, *Reasoning with God: Reclaiming Shariah in the Modern Age* (Lanham, MD: Rowman and Littlefield, 2014), 306.

23. Abou El Fadl, 306.

24. Abou El Fadl, 322–24.

25. Khaled Abou El Fadl, "Violence, Personal Commitment and Democracy," in *Islam and English Law: Rights, Responsibilities and the Place of Shari'a,* ed. Robin Griffith-Jones (Cambridge: Cambridge University Press, 2013), 271.

26. Murad Hofmann, "Governing under Islam and the Islamic Political System," *American Journal of Islamic Social Sciences* 18, no. 3 (2001): 1–16.

27. Hofmann, 11.

28. Louay M. Safi, "Overcoming the Religious-Secular Divide: Islam's Contribution to Civilization," in *Muslim Contributions to World Civilization,* ed. M. Basheer Ahmed, Syed A. Ahsani, and Dilnawaz A. Siddiqui (London: International Institute of Islamic Thought, 2011), 7, 12–13, 17. Reproduced with written permission by the Publisher and copyrights holder: The International Institute of Islamic Thought (IIIT).

29. Safi, 21.

30. Safi, 21.

31. Safi, 21–22.

32. Shabbir Akhtar, *Islam as Political Religion: The Future of an Imperial Faith* (London: Routledge, 2011), 8.

Islamic Texts on Ideals and Realities of Muslim Community Ordering

The Muslim Community in Relation to the Creator:
Obedience and Servitude

Surat al-Taghabun [64]:12

Obey God and obey His messenger. If you turn away, then the duty of Our messenger is only to convey the message plainly.

Surat al-Dhariyat [51]:56–58

[56]I created jinn and humankind only that they might worship Me. [57]I seek no livelihood from them, nor do I ask that they should feed Me. [58]Indeed, God is the Provider, the Possessor of Power, the Unbreakably Mighty.

The Muslim Community in Relation to Other Creatures:
Stewardship and Subjugation

Surat al-Baqara [2]:30

[Remember] when your Lord said to the angels, "Indeed, I am about to place a vicegerent on earth," they said, "Will you place there someone who will do harm and will shed blood, while we, we hymn Your praise and sanctify You?" He said, "Surely I know that which you know not."

Surat al-An'am [6]:165

He it is Who has placed you as vicegerents of the earth and has exalted some of you in rank above others, that He may try you by (the test of) that which He hath given you. Indeed, your Lord is swift in prosecution; and, indeed, He truly is Forgiving, Merciful.

Hadith

Al-Muttaqi al-Hindi, *Kanz al-Ummal*[1]

He who enjoins good (*ma'ruf*) and prohibits evil (*munkar*) is the vicegerent (*khalifa*) of Allah, the Qur'an, and the Prophet on the Earth.

Surat al-Jathiya [45]:13

He has made of service to you whatsoever is in the heavens and whatsoever is in the earth; it is all from Him. Indeed, in this are signs for a people who reflect.

Inner Life and Ordering of the Muslim Community

General Observations
Surat al-Anfal [8]:73

The disbelievers are protectors of one another. If you do not do likewise, there will be confusion in the land and great corruption.

Surat al-Tawba [9]:71

The believers, both men and women, are the protecting friends of one another; they enjoin the right and forbid what is wrong.

Surat al-Hujurat [49]:9-10

[9]If two parties of believers fall to fighting [each other], then try to make peace between them. And if one party does wrong to the other, fight the wrongdoers until they submit to God's command; then, if they return, make peace between them justly, and act equitably. Indeed, God loves the equitable. [10]The believers are nothing but brothers. Therefore, make peace between your brethren and be mindful of your duty to God, so that perhaps you may receive mercy

Hadith

Sahih al-Bukhari 5665; Sahih Muslim 2586

An-Nu'man ibn Basheer reported: The Messenger of God, peace and blessings be upon him, said, "The parable of the believers in their affection, mercy, and compassion for each other is that of a body. When any limb aches, the whole body reacts with sleeplessness and fever."

Exemplary community

Surat al-Baqara [2]:143a

We have appointed you [as] a middle nation, so that you may be witnesses against humankind, and so that the messenger may be a witness against you.

Surat Āl ʿImran [3]:102–105

[102]O you who believe! Be dutiful to God with proper observance, and do not die except in a state of submission to Him. [103]Hold fast, all of you together, to the cable of God, and do not split up. Remember God's favor to you: How you were enemies and He brought your hearts together so that you became as brothers by His grace; and (how) you were on the brink of an abyss of fire, and He saved you from it. Thus, God makes clear His revelations to you, that perhaps you may be guided, [104]and there may spring from you a nation that invites goodness and enjoins right conduct and forbids indecency. They who are the successful ones. [105]Do not be like those who split into factions and disputed with one another even after clear revelation had come to them. For such people there is an awful doom.

Surat Āl ʿImran [3]:110

You are the best community that has been raised up for humankind. You enjoin right conduct and forbid the wrong; and you believe in God. If the People of the Book had believed, it would have been better for them. Some of them are believers; but most of them are wicked.

Hadith

Sunan al-Tirmidhi, no. 5142

Once the Angel Jibreel (peace be upon him) was sent by God (peace be upon him) to destroy a town. Jibreel (peace be upon him) asked if the pious man in the town, who spent his every moment in the remembrance of God, was also meant to be destroyed. God (peace be upon him) told him to annihilate that "pious" man first, since he did not bother to guide his people.

Surat al-Maʾida [5]:54–56

[54]O you who believe! If any of you becomes a renegade from his religion, (know that in your stead) God will bring a people whom He loves and who love Him, humble toward believers, stern toward disbelievers, striving in the way of God, and fearing not the blame of any blamer. Such is the grace of God which He gives to whomever He will. God is All-Embracing, All-Knowing. [55]Your guardian can be only God; and His messenger and those who believe, who perform prayer and

pay the alms tax, and bow down (in worship). [56]And whosoever takes God and His messenger and those who believe for protection (will know that), indeed: the party of God, they are the victorious

Authority and the Proper Exercise of Power/Good Governance
Surat al-Shura [42]:36-43

[36]Whatever you have been given is but a passing comfort for the life of this world. What God has is better and more lasting for those who believe and put their trust in the Lord, [37]and those who shun the worst of sins and indecencies and—when they are angry—forgive, [38]and those who answer the call of their Lord and perform prayer, and whose affairs are a matter of counsel, and who spend of what We have bestowed on them, [39]and those who—when great wrong is done to them—defend themselves. [40]The recompence of an ill-deed is an ill similar to it. But whosoever pardons and makes amends, his wage is the affair of God. Indeed, He loves not wrong-doers. [41]And whoever defends himself after he has suffered wrong—for such, there is no way (of blame) against them. [42]The way (of blame) is only against those who oppress humankind, and wrongfully rebel in the earth. For such there is a painful doom.[43] And whoever is patient and forgives—that, indeed, is (of) the steadfast heart of things.

Surat al-Nisa' [4]:135, 139

[135]O you who believe! Be staunch in justice, witnesses for God, even though it be against yourselves or your parents or your kindred. Whether the case be of a rich person or a poor person, God is nearer to both (than you are). . . . [139]Those who choose disbelievers for their allies instead of believers: do they seek power at their hands? Indeed, all power belongs to God

Surat al-Munafiqun [63]:8

They say, "Surely, if we return to Medina the mightier will soon drive out the weaker." Yet might belongs to God, and to His messenger, and to the believers; but the hypocrites know not.

Surat al-Nisa' [4]:58-59

[58]Indeed, God commands you to restore deposits to their rightful owners and, if you judge between people, that you judge justly. Indeed, excellent is this which God admonishes you. Indeed, God is ever Hearer, Seer. [59]O you who believe! Obey God and obey the messenger and those of you who are in authority; and if you have a dispute concerning any matter, refer it to God and the

messenger—if you truly are believers in God and the Last Day. That is better and fairer in the end.

Hadith

Jamiʿ al-Tirmidhi

"Do not be blind followers. Do not say: if people do good I will join them in doing good and if they do bad we join them, but be of principle. When people do good you do good as well but when people do wrong you should not join them."

"There is no obedience to the creation in disobedience to God." ("There is no obedience to men in disobedience to God; obedience is due in *ma'ruf* things.")

Abu Bakr, from his inaugural speech:

I have been appointed as ruler over you, though I am not the best of you. If I do well (to you) then you should support me, and if I do evil (to you) then you should guide me to what is right. . . . Behold! The weak person amongst you should be considered as strong in my sight until I bring back to him his right (usurped by others). Behold! The strong person among you should be considered as weak in my sight until I take from him the right of others, which he usurped. You should obey me as long as I comply with (the orders and instructions of) God and His Messenger. But, if I deviate (from that), then you should have the right not to obey me.[2]

Muhammad al-Shahrastani

When the death of Abu Bakr (may God be pleased with him) neared he said (to the companions), "Consult amongst yourselves about this matter (of caliphate)." He then described the attributes of Umar (praising him) and chose him as successor. It did not occur to his heart, or that of anyone else, in the least, that it is permissible for there to be no imam. When the death of Umar (may God be pleased with him) neared he made the matter one of consultation between six, and they consented upon Uthman, and after that upon Ali. All of this indicates that the companions, the first and best of the Muslims, consented that having an imam was necessary. . . . This type of consensus is a definitive evidence for the obligation of the imamah.[3]

Hadith

Sahih Muslim 2664

A strong believer is better and is more lovable to God than a weak believer, and there is good in everyone.

Surat al-Nisa' [4]:97–98

[97]As for those whom the angels take (in death) while they wrong themselves, (the angels) will ask them, "In what were you engaged?" They will answer, "We were oppressed in the land." (The angels) will say, "Was not God's earth spacious enough that you could have migrated therein?" For such, their habitation will be hell, an evil journey's end; [98]except for the feeble among the men, women, and children, who are unable to devise a plan and are not shown a way out.

Surat al-Anbiya' [21]:105

Indeed, We have written in the Psalms, after the Reminder: "My righteous servants will inherit the earth."

Ayatullah Ruhullah Khumayni on Islamic Government

They ["the enemies"] have said that Islam has no relationship whatsoever with organizing life and society or with creating a government of any kind and that it only concerns itself with the rules of menstruation and childbirth. It may contain some ethics. But beyond this, it has no bearing on issues of life and of organizing society. It is regrettable that all this has had its bad effect not only on the ordinary people but also among college people and the students of theology. They misunderstand Islam and are ignorant of it. . . .

Because Islam is immortal, it must be implemented and observed forever. If what was permissible by Muhammad is permissible until the day of resurrection, then Muhammad's restrictions must not be suspended, his teachings must not be neglected, punishment must not be abandoned, tax collection must not be stopped and defense of the nation of the Muslims and of their lands must not be abandoned. The belief that Islam came for a limited period and for a certain place violates the essentials of the Islamic beliefs. Considering that the implementation forever of laws after the venerable prophet, may God's prayers be upon him, is one of the essentials of life, then it is necessary for government to exist and for this government to have the qualities of an executive and administrative authority. Without this, social chaos, corruption and ideological and moral deviation would prevail. This can be prevented only through the creation of a just government that runs all aspects of life . . . .

If a knowledgeable and just jurisprudent undertakes the task of forming the government, then he will run the social affairs that the prophet used to run and it is the duty of the people to listen to him and obey him.

This ruler will have as much control over running the people's administration, welfare, and policy as the prophet and Amir of the faithful had despite the special virtues and the traits that distinguished the prophet and the Imam. Their virtues did not entitle them to contradict the instructions of the Sharia or to dominate people with disregard to God's order.[4]

Abdullahi Ahmed An-Na'im on Islam and the Secular State

In order to be a Muslim by conviction and free choice, which is the only way one can be a Muslim, I need a secular state. By a secular state I mean one that is neutral regarding religious doctrine, one that does not claim or pretend to enforce Shari'a—the religious law of Islam—simply because compliance with Shari'a cannot be coerced by fear of state institutions or faked to appease officials. This is what I mean by secularism in this book, namely, a secular state that facilitates the possibility of religious piety out of honest conviction. My call for the state, and not society, to be secular is intended to enhance and promote genuine religious observance, to affirm, nurture, and regulate the role of Islam in the public life of the community. Conversely, I will argue that the claim of a so-called Islamic state to coercively enforce Shari'a repudiates the foundational role of Islam in the socialization of children and the sanctification of social institutions and relationships. When observed voluntarily, Shari'a plays a fundamental role in shaping and developing ethical norms and values that can be reflected in general legislation and public policy through the democratic political process. But I will argue in this book that Shari'a principles cannot be enacted and enforced by the state as public law and public policy solely on the grounds that they are believed to be part of Shari'a. If such enactment and enforcement is attempted, the outcome will necessarily be the political will of the state and not the religious law of Islam.[5]

Notes

In this chapter, all passages from the Qur'an are according to Mohammed Marmaduke Pickthall, *The Meaning of the Glorious Qur'ān* (London: Knopf, 1930), adapted slightly.

1. In this chapter, all hadiths have been translated by members of the Building Bridges Seminar.

2. *Al-Bidāyah wa'l-Nihāyah* 6:305, 306. Translated by members of the Building Bridges Seminar.

3. Translated by members of the Building Bridges Seminar. Muhamad al-Shahrastani (1086–1153), of Persia, was an esteemed and influential philosopher and theologian.

4. Ayatullah Ruhullah Khumayni, *Islamic Government* [*Vilayat-i Faqih*], trans. Joint Publications Research Service (Arlington, VA: National Technical Information Service, 1979), 1a–3, 10, 13–14, 17, 20–22. The author's name is often transliterated Ayatollah Ruhollah Khomeini. He was the leader of the 1979 Iranian Revolution that established Iran as an Islamic republic. For Hamid Algar's translation of this work, see http://www.iran chamber.com/history/rkhomeini/books/velayat_faqeeh.pdf, accessed May 25, 2019.

5. Abdullahi Ahmed An-Na'im, *Islam and the Secular State: Negotiating the Future of Shari'a* (Cambridge, MA: Harvard University Press, 2008), 1; © 2008 by the President and Fellows of Harvard College. Used by permission.

From Nation to Church

The Community of God's Rule

JOAN O'DONOVAN

As the texts selected for discussion during Building Bridges Seminar 2017, and included in this volume, abundantly show, Christianity and Islam share a fundamental premise: that God's revealed power is coterminous with his sovereign creation of the world and sovereign rule over his creation. The texts which I introduce in this essay are principally concerned with God's revealed power in ruling his elect people; the principal aim of my introduction is to situate these texts within a coherent account of the history of human mediation of God's rule and the corresponding promise and reality of communal identity and action. In the biblical writings, the two foci of this history—the history of Israel in the Old Testament and of Jesus Christ in the New—display both continuity and discontinuity; for the history of Christ is not only the climax but a new chapter of the history of God's rule: its final and pivotal mediation determining the past and future of his people, and, through them, of humanity and the nonhuman creation.

Nevertheless, the two historical foci exhibit many parallels. In both, God rules by gathering his people; by delivering them from bondage; by giving judgment for his people, against his people, and among his people; by commanding them to action, promulgating his commands as law, and empowering their obedient response; by receiving the homage of his people in acts of worship (of praise, thanksgiving, recollection, repentance, and petition); and by promising them an eternally secure future of common fulfillment. In both, a single mediator comprehensively represents the royal, priestly, and prophetic dimensions of the corporate identity of God's people under his rule.

The Mediation of Moses and the Covenantal Law of the Israelite Nation

The book of Deuteronomy, presenting a prominent strand of Judean reforming theology from the seventh to the fifth centuries BCE, anchors Israel's legal tradition firmly in the unitary, comprehensive mediation of God's rule by Moses. Its introductory chapters (1–3) present Moses as the instrument and mouthpiece of God's deliverance of Israel from Egyptian bondage, of God's judgments against Egypt and for Israel, and of God's judgment against rebellious Israel in the wilderness. The chapters present Moses as intercessor with God for his people's defections and as organizer of their worship. Finally, they present him as promulgator of God's gracious covenantal law at Sinai (the Decalogue) and its fuller unfolding in stipulations for his people's settled communal life in the land which they are occupying as his unmerited gift.

The Deuteronomic laws purport to be these stipulations expounded by Moses to the Israelite tribes poised to take possession by conquest of the Promised Land west of the Jordan, having already taken possession of territory east of the Jordan. Israel's obedience to them is, therefore, the practical form of the nation's adherence to God's covenant of election: it is Israel's testimony of praise and thanksgiving to the sovereign creator who has delivered this people from enslavement and promised to prosper their communal life in righteousness so that they may perpetually show forth his generosity, faithfulness, righteousness, and justice. Israel's continuing prosperity in the land is entirely dependent on the people's whole-hearted devotion and obedience, expressed primarily in the spiritual and ritual purity of her monotheistic worship but also in every aspect of her political, social, and economic organization.

The "laws of release" given in Deuteronomy 15, covering release from debt (1–11) and from debt slavery (12–18), exhibit two characteristic features of the Deuteronomic laws: they are wide-ranging in accommodating urban as well as agrarian needs, and they give evidence of extending, reinterpreting, and adding to older legal material.[1] It is significant that they are framed by laws of sacrificial, ceremonial tithing that closely link devotion to Yahweh with providing for the Levitical priests and for the needy poor. Additionally, a related law of Sabbath rest for the land, releasing it from cultivation every seven years (Exod. 23:10–11), is similarly concerned with providing for the poor and for grazing beasts as well.

While the precise obligations placed on creditors by the law of debt release are a matter of scholarly debate, the purpose of the law of release is the immediate relief and future welfare of the impoverished debtor, which also must be the creditor's primary motive for lending.[2] The creditor's "free," "ungrudging" lending expresses his profound spiritual embrace of Yahweh's will that all Israelite brothers enjoy his covenantal gift of the land and the attendant blessings promised by him (Deut. 15:4–5). Consequently, the law of septennial debt release, like the law prohibiting interest on loans, does not apply to foreign debtors who have no direct portion in Yahweh's gift and promises to Israel. Indeed, Yahweh's blessings on his obedient people include the national prosperity flowing from commercial lending at interest to foreign traders.

Another blessing flowing from the practice of septennial debt release may be the absence of a large class of debt slaves: of those poor who, defaulting on payment, become caught in a spiral of ever more punitive loan conditions, terminating in loss of property and servitude. The presence in Israel of debt servitude is addressed by the following law of septennial release, which shares with the law of debt release the moral and social imperative to restore impoverished individuals and families to a more fulfilling, propertied role in communal life.

Importantly, a later redaction of Deuteronomy after the fall of Jerusalem in 587 BCE incorporates a prophetic foretelling of God's depriving his people of the land and the associated blessings of national life in chastisement for their repeated and long-standing violations of his covenant law and, eventually, God's restoring a chastened and repentant people to their promised patrimony and national prosperity. Other prophetic voices of the periods of Israelite exile and partial restoration in the land exemplify a different tendency: namely, to detach Israel's obedient love and service of God from the traditional authorities, institutions, and practices of communal justice, worship, and instruction, and to focus, rather, on solitary individuals whom God has brought through extreme suffering and social isolation—through anger, doubt, and despair over his justice; through fear of physical dissolution and death—to confess his faithfulness and to entrust themselves to his unfailing love. These are the anguished voices of Job, of the psalms of lament, of the lone prophet Jeremiah who bears before God in his suffering conscience the sins and the misery of his chastised brethren, only to be despised and persecuted by them—a figure closely resonating with the "suffering servant" of the Isaiah passage 52:13–53:3.

The Mediation of Jesus Christ: From Pre-Resurrection Discipleship to Post-Resurrection Fellowship of Believers

Only in the history of Jesus, recapitulating the history of Israel, is the unitary, comprehensive mediation of God's rule by a single individual restored to his people and, through them, to all humanity and the whole of creation. The key to the finality and perfection of Jesus's mediation of God's rule, and to the communal renewal it inaugurates, is the unique, unprecedented relation of Jesus to God as Father and as Spirit—a relation that is so intimate, so fathomless and all-embracing, that the history of Jesus manifests God's acting as Son and as Spirit. The climactic revelation of Jesus's sonship—his obedient suffering unto death and resurrection to glory—is the climactic revelation of God gracious judgment on his sinful people, which is their final, irreversible reconciliation, vindication, and justification.

Sacrificially suffering his Father's righteous judgment on human sin, the crucified Son, by his resurrection and exaltation, is shown to be the wholly acceptable offering for sin and the high priest worthy of making intercession for sinners. Wholly vindicated of sin and guilt, his obedience proved, the royal Son and Servant is worthy to pronounce his Father's judgment on the guilty and to command the faithful obedience of his servants with divine authority. Having overcome the constraining and condemning rule of God's righteous law over sinful humanity, he has opened the way for a free and joyful human service of his Father's will. Having broken the bondage of death, the risen Son has saved his people from the final death of being eternally cut off from God and has sealed God's promise of an everlasting covenant community radiating the glory of his rule by pouring his own Spirit of truth, love, and holiness on his followers, binding them together in fellowship with God and with one another.[3]

All the interpretative accounts of the history of Jesus's mediation of God's rule found in the New Testament are post-resurrection, being written for dispersed groups of believers in the resurrection victory of their crucified Lord. Whether Gospels or letters, they all depend on earlier and firsthand sources for the earthly life and ministry of Jesus prior to his resurrection appearances, while at the same time, they are all concerned with the immediate task of recruiting and building up fellow believers in the saving truth of Christ. Naturally, there are some shifts of style and perspective between the Gospel narratives of Jesus's pre-resurrection history and the more coherent and synthetic theological instruction of the letters. Nonetheless, in their different ways, they all contribute to the mature vision of a united community of God's rule in Jesus Christ through the Holy Spirit: a commonwealth of repentant faith in the Father's reconciling judgment of sinners in his Son; hope in the promised perfecting of human knowledge, freedom, and love in Christ's eternal kingdom; and striving in the power of the Spirit to perform works of loving service to God and neighbor.

The author of the Gospel of Luke and its sequel, the book of Acts (whose traditional identification as the fellow evangelist and sometimes companion of the apostle Paul continues to have strong scholarly support), provides the only narrative account bridging the original gathering of messianic disciples around Jesus and the gathering and growth after his ascension of fledgling communities of believers in Jesus. Controlling his extended historical narrative of the genesis and growth of the Christian fellowship or church (*ecclesia*), probably written in the 80s CE for a Gentile patron and congregation, is Luke's conviction of "the gracious outreach and wide embrace" of God's coming kingdom realized through Jesus.[4] By his teaching, promises, and miracles, Jesus brings messianic release to people trapped in miserable bondage, overthrowing the myriad powers depriving them of the fullness of life that God wills for them. His compassionate acceptance is especially extended to the poor and despised, occupying the fringes of Israelite society, whose material and social suffering heightens their receptivity to Jesus's summons to repentance and newness of life (see Luke 4:18–19; 6:20–21). Conversely, material riches are to Luke's Jesus a particular obstacle to such receptivity in that they foster in those who pursue or possess them a posture of callous self-seeking and complacent self-sufficiency (see Luke 16:1–15, 19–31; 12:13–34).

Finally, Luke presents Jesus as exceeding the eschatological prophets of Israel in his total possession by God's Spirit and his complete revelation of God's kingdom in word and deed, both of which are aspects of his unique relationship to God as son to father.

For Luke the pivotal expression by Jesus of his unique sonship is his prayerful address to God as "Father": *patēr* in Greek, widely taken by scholars to translate the Aramaic *abbâ* used by Jesus (as attested by Mark's Gospel [14:36] and implied by Paul's letters [Gal. 4:6; Rom. 8:17]). It is this intimate filial address of *abbâ/ patēr*, rather than the more formal "Our Father" (*abinu*) of contemporary Jewish usage, that Luke's Jesus gives to his disciples in teaching them to pray. Some scholars take this as evidence of Luke's drawing on an earlier account of Jesus's instruction than informs Matthew's longer, fuller prayer retaining the more formal "Our Father," which, however, proved better suited to the common worship of Christian assemblies.

To the sonship of Jesus, then, belongs the authority to communicate sonship, that is, to reveal that relation to God as Father that only he as Son knows. By introducing his disciples to his own prayer, Jesus shares with them his lived relationship to his heavenly Father and invites them to be conformed to it.[5] In the prayer's petitions, he discloses the yearnings, expectations, and attitudes appropriate to their sonship. They are to yearn for and expectantly await universal human acknowledgement of the Father's true nature and willing subjection to his transforming rule. They are to be utterly dependent on the Father's provision of daily sustenance to his children. They are to be ever conscious of their need for the Father's forgiveness and, inseparably, for the spirit of forgiveness within themselves. (Can it be that receiving forgiveness and forgiving others is by the same Spirit?) Finally, they are to be aware of their moral frailty, of their need to be protected from the perilous testing that temptation (*peirasmos*) is, or alternatively, from "entering into temptation," that is, from succumbing to the seductive evil that temptation presents (Luke 22:46).

The subtle interdependence of asking and receiving, seeking and finding in Jesus's exhortation to persevere in prayer terminates in his assurance of the Father's gift of the Holy Spirit: that is, of God's own power enabling faithful human response to him and faithful witness to his coming kingdom. We hear echoes of Paul's assurance that "when we cry *Abba! Father!* it is the Spirit himself bearing witness with our spirit that we are children of God [by adoption] and heirs. . . with Christ" of the future resurrection life of God's creation (Rom. 8:16–17; also Gal. 4:6). Although Luke, unlike Paul, does not in this passage explicitly identify the Spirit who bears witness as the Spirit both of the Father and of his risen and exalted Son, he makes this identification with dramatic force in the opening chapters of Acts where he testifies that Jesus Christ's departure to reign with his heavenly Father issues in his unprecedented outpouring of the Holy Spirit on the apostles (Acts 2:33; cf. John 7:39; 16:7).

Immediately preceding the apostle Peter's lengthy oration (Acts 2:14–36), Luke presents the ascended Christ's outpouring of his Spirit as "a major theophanic event" occurring on the Jewish Day of Pentecost, on which was celebrated the theophany at Mount Sinai and God's giving of the law to Israel.[6] Accordingly, as God's promulgation of his law was the foundation and engine of Israel's faithful and obedient communal witness to his rule, so God's outpouring of his Spirit is the foundation and engine of the faithful and obedient witness of Christ's community of discipleship to his coming rule. Its immediate effect is the apostles' proclamation of God's great deeds in Jesus to a linguistically diverse crowd of Jews in an ecstatic speech that, for some listeners, overcomes all barriers of linguistic incomprehension, so reversing that "confusion of tongues" which, according to one strand of interpreting Genesis 11:1–9, constituted God's punishment of the hubris of a linguistically united humanity.

The apostle Peter's subsequent oration (concluding at v. 36), and exhortations (vv. 37–40), show this twofold miracle of speech and hearing to be paradigmatic for the apostles' mission and for the mission of Christ's faithful community, for the Spirit renders Peter's testimony to God's exultation of the crucified Jesus powerful in impelling those who hear to accept Jesus as Israel's messiah, repent of their sins, and undergo baptism in Christ's name "for the forgiveness" of their sins. The first speech act of the Messiah's followers is, then, proclamation of what God has accomplished in him; the second is ritual washing of the newly converted in Christ's name[7]—a symbolic combining of speech and physical act that, Luke indicates, is powerful in bringing about what it signifies, being an effectual seal or pledge of God's forgiveness of the sins of penitent believers in Jesus and his promised gift of the Spirit. More frequently, we should note, New Testament passages stress the presence of God's Spirit in the baptismal rite as both gift received and divine agent, achieving the inward operation of regeneration of which washing is the outward sign (see, e.g., John 3:5; 1 Cor. 12:13; Titus 3:5). The original example of the Spirit's baptismal presence is, however, his palpable descent on Jesus as he ascended from the water of baptism (see Matt. 3:16; Luke 3:22; cf. John 1:32–34), testifying not to his regeneration but to the unique endowment of the Father's Son with his Spirit.

Among the core activities of the nascent church—those of prayer, worship, and attending to the apostles' teaching—Luke mentions the second core cultic rite of Christian fellowship: namely, "the breaking of bread," widely understood by scholars to be a formulaic expression for the early form of the "Lord's Supper" set out by Paul in his first letter to the Corinthian congregation. Paul connects this rite with Jesus's actions and instructions during his Passover meal with his disciples immediately preceding his "passion," so that after his earthly departure, his faithful followers would participate in his sacrificial suffering and death, as in his resurrection to glory, by partaking together of bread and wine (1 Cor. 11:19). Significantly for Christian tradition, Paul regarded both baptism and the Lord's Supper as special vehicles of the Spirit's action, knitting believers together in communion with Christ in his saving acts and in mutual enjoyment of the spiritual fruits of Christ's acts—those of faith, hope, and love—imparted to them as God's adopted Sons with Christ (see 1 Cor. 10:14–18; Col. 2:12–13; Gal. 3:26–27).

Also of importance for Christian tradition is Luke's report that the common sharing of new believers in the spiritual blessings of prayer, praise, thanksgiving, and sacramental celebration is accompanied by their common sharing of material blessings: "All who believed were together and had all things in common" (2:44). Luke influentially expands his report in Acts 4:32–37: "Now the company of those who believed were of one heart and soul, and no one said that any of the things which he possessed was his own, but they had everything in common" (4:32). "There was not a needy person among them, for as many as were possessors of lands or houses sold them, and brought the proceeds of what was sold and laid it at the apostles' feet; and distribution was made to each as any had need" (4:34–35). Christian interpretations of this communal sharing of material goods have disagreed as to whether it took the form of charitable distribution of believers' superfluous wealth, collective ownership of property, or even common use of goods without individual or collective ownership of them. Without deciding this issue, it should be said that until the twelfth century CE, Christian thinkers widely regarded the acquisition and possession of material goods by legal title (i.e., property) as morally ambiguous and not merely the selfish amassing of wealth, persuaded that the sharing of divisible material goods among believers should correspond to and support their sharing of indivisible spiritual goods as much as was practically possible. This was an eschatological witness within Christ's earthly communion to the future perfecting restoration in his kingdom of created humankind's sharing of the gifts of God in nature. Possessed by God in Christ through the Spirit and possessing God in Christ through the Spirit, the faithful possess themselves, one another, and the nonhuman creation in the knowledge and love of God so that their communion is an unceasing communication of his spiritual and material blessings.

The Gospel of Matthew was as influential as Luke's writings in anchoring the ethos and practical discipline of the post-resurrection community of believers in Jesus in the recorded deeds and words of their Master's earthly ministry; but its author brings to this undertaking a somewhat different orientation, commonly thought by scholars to be that of a Jewish Christian, writing for a mainly Jewish fellowship of believers in Jesus the Messiah during the period of rabbinic consolidation of Jewish communal life around the synagogue and legal tradition, following the sacking and destruction of Jerusalem and the second temple in 70 CE. To the contemporary enterprise of rabbinical Judaism, Matthew's Gospel stands in a close, if somewhat polemical, relation. Owing to its apologetic value in demonstrating the history of Jesus to be the fulfillment of the ancient Jewish Messianic prophecies and its pedagogical effectiveness in shaping the common Christian life and mission, this work was favored reading in both the Jewish and Gentile churches of the early centuries.

The Davidic messianic kingship of Jesus prominent in the Gospel is cast in the images of shepherding and servanthood, demonstrating a striking combination of commanding royal authority and condescending humility, gentleness, loving-kindness, magnanimity, merciful justice, and compassion. These latter qualities must likewise characterize the spirit and action of the Messiah's would-be subjects, as Matthew's version of the Beatitudes in 5:1–10 luminously conveys. Conversely, the proud, mean, uncharitable, and negligent spirit attracts the most vigorous condemnation (as, e.g., in the singular account of the Son of Man's eschatological assize in Matt. 25:31–46).

Central to Matthew's robust ethical orientation is his confidence that the commands have the power to elicit obedience from those who believe that in him God's covenant promises grounding Israel's communal law are being fulfilled. This confidence underpins Matthew's presentation of the sustained, paradigmatic radicalizing of the Mosaic law by Jesus (Matt. 5:17–6:18), demonstrating how the righteousness that he commands of his disciples exceeds or surpasses in every injunction that of "the scribes and Pharisees" (Matt. 5:17–20). Late in the sequence of uncompromising commands followed by severe warnings is this: "Judge not, that you be not judged. For with the judgment you pronounce you will be judged" (Matt. 7:1–2a).

It is hardly surprising, then, that the account of fraternal correction and reproof offered in Matthew 18:15–22 should be embedded in the Lord's exacting summons of his disciples to relations of childlike humility, unstinting affection and consideration for the meek and vulnerable (including children), and incalculable forgiveness (Matt. 18:1–14, 21–22). Believers are exhorted to take perpetual care, lest in their corrupt conceit they tempt the immature and simple of faith to sin (Matt. 18:5–7, 10). Only a fellowship of the spiritually disciplined can undertake with integrity the task of judging offenses committed by its members. The disciplinary procedure laid down by Jesus demonstrates that its aim throughout is repentance and reconciliation of offender and offended, with exclusion of the offender from the company of believers being the outcome of his stubborn "refusal to listen" to patient and weighty admonition. While it is clear that the community's judgment of exclusion carries heavenly authority and expresses Christ's presence among his people (18:18–20), its eschatological significance is not, on that account, transparent; for the judgment may be a sign of God's eschatological judgment without being a determination of it. What is clear is the dramatic tension between the unbounded requirement on the individual disciple to forgive and forbear offending brothers (driven home with more terrifying severity in the concluding parable of the unmerciful servant in 18:23–35) and the responsibility of the fellowship to sustain the integrity of its messianic witness.

The same tension between the imperatives to forgive and forebear injuries, on the one hand, and to discipline wrongdoers, on the other, is equally striking in the apostle Paul's letters to the communities of Christ's followers in Corinth, Rome, and Galatia.[8] In Paul's thought, this tension is embedded within his vision of the controlling power and action of the Holy Spirit within and through the fellowship of believers, to which we must first attend. Turning specifically to his letters to the Corinthians and the Romans, we see that, for Paul, the Holy Spirit is the Spirit of the Son and of the Father, who unites sinful humanity with the Father's saving work of reconciliation and justification accomplished in Jesus Christ. Pivotally, the Spirit enables members of Christ's fellowship to participate, through faith and hope, in the freedom and love of their crucified, risen, and exalted Savior, therein renewing their thinking and their acting.

As Paul, like Luke, conceives the earthly fellowship of Christ's faithful as an *ekklēsia*—a local "congregation" or "assembly" of believers—the renewed powers of thinking and acting imparted by the Holy Spirit are primarily for, on behalf of, and within the local congregation, contributing to the growth of each and all of its members in faith, hope, and love. However, as the local congregation is a missionary congregation, continually drawing in new believers, and as its members are individually and collectively interacting in myriad ways with nonbelievers, Jews and Gentiles, regularly experiencing their hostility and violence at the personal and institutional levels, the believers' powers of acting have an expansive, indefinite social horizon. Crucially, the special vocation of apostles is to travel far and wide, bringing into being and nurturing new communities of believers by the action of God's Spirit working through their special gifts of preaching, teaching, leading, and pastoral care; testifying thereby that God's salvation in Christ, as achieved reality and promised future, embraces the whole of humanity and the created world, the perplexing mystery being the apparent human failure to embrace salvation.

Most influential for New Testament ethics, Paul conceives the generative power and action of the Holy Spirit in terms of love. Love (*agapē, agapeo*) is the unifying and ordering power of the individual and communal moral life of believers, being an orientation of the "mind" and the "heart," of the individual's most profound discernment, affections, desiring, and resolve. Originating in the divine relationship of Father and Son, love is uniquely revealed in the incarnate Son's reconciliation of sinful humanity to his Father by suffering unto death God's righteous judgment on human sin. All sinners who are united by faith with Christ's reconciling death and resurrection life and who hope for the fulfillment of eternal communion with God thereby participate in God's love. Their love is faith and hope in action, communicating God's love by the power of his Spirit.

Their love always has a twofold direction: toward God and toward the neighbor, in obedience to the twofold command of Jesus in the synoptic Gospels, which combine the rule of worship given in Deuteronomy 6:5 ("you shall love the Lord your God with all your heart, and with all your soul, and with all your might") with the rule of social life given in Leviticus 19:18 ("you shall love your neighbor as yourself").[9] Both the unity and the twofold direction of the love commanded manifest the origin and perfection of human love in God. Nevertheless, in explicating the moral territory ruled by love, Paul gives most prominence to love for the neighbor, as do the testimonies of the four Gospels to Jesus's teaching and works.

In Paul's letter of 52–53 CE to the Corinthian church that he had founded several years earlier, the territory ruled by love is the *ekklēsia*, the congregation of believers. Paul's concern in 1 Corinthians 12 (the chapter preceding his celebrated "ode to love") is to clarify the nature of community in the Holy Spirit as manifesting both the diversity of gifts and services contributed by its members and their unity of belonging to one Lord. Responding to reports that some members of the Corinthian church have been displaying elitist, partisan conduct and social hubris, exalting their own spiritual capacities (especially of "wisdom" and "tongues") to the disparagement of other members, Paul instructs them that, under Christ's lordship, individual members place their gifts at the disposal of all, undertake their service for the common benefit, and honor and cherish equally the contributions of each and every member. Balancing the equality in estimation of every contribution, Paul indicates a divinely appointed order of service for the welfare of Christ's body, at the head of which is the service of the apostle, followed by the prophet, and the teacher, all of which are most crucial to uniting the congregation "in the same mind and the same judgment" (1 Cor. 1:10).[10] These sustain the spiritual framework within which "workers of miracles, . . . healers, helpers, administrators, speakers in various kinds of tongues" (1 Cor. 12:28) bestow the benefit of their gifts on fellow believers and take forward the church's mission.

Paul's later letter of the mid-50s CE to the Roman church again portrays its members—Jews and Gentiles—as forming "one body in Christ" and as "individually members one of another" (Rom. 12:5). Here their unifying bond of love is not only to be expressed within the fellowship in "brotherly affection," humility and mutual deference, generosity, hospitality, and prayer; it is also to be expressed within and beyond the fellowship in blessing one's persecutors, repaying no one "evil for evil" (Rom. 12:17), never avenging injuries to oneself but rather giving one's enemies cause for repentance by acting charitably toward them (heaping burning coals on their heads, in Paul's graphic phrase)—in short, by always "overcom[ing] evil with good" (Rom. 12:21).

The attention given to the imperatives not to judge others, not to seek vengeance but to forgive injuries, within Paul's exhortations regarding the individual and communal moral life of believers expresses his pivotal conviction that judgment over the faithful belongs exclusively to God in Christ, who is both "the judge" and "the judged." As the faithful are already reconciled to God and renewed in the Spirit through Christ's righteousness, they have no need of human condemnation and vindication, including the vindication provided by legal redress for wrongs suffered (1 Cor. 6:7). Consequently, the vindication and condemnation of public judgment occupies no place among the sanctifying services performed for Christ's fellowship by its members. Indeed, in Romans 13:1–7, set in deliberate counterpoint to his unfolding of love's ethos in Christ's fellowship, Paul makes coercive judgment the constitutive feature of secular political authority and law. By describing the remit of secular rule as that of executing God's wrath on the wrongdoer, Paul indicates, at the same time, that secular rule has a divinely authorized and indispensable worldly role in combating sin's ravages in human society and that it can never be more than a remote and deficient sign and agent of the Holy Spirit's work of unifying reconciled humanity in the truth of Christ's rule.

Nevertheless, as still struggling under the legacy of sin, the faithful continue to need loving correction and reproof within their fellowship, even terminating in expulsion of the impenitent offender, should the integrity of their common faith and love require it (1 Cor. 5:9–13). Answering this need, the apostles' service to the church is one of superior public authority: rooted in their unique, founding commission from the risen Christ, its scope is disciplinary as well as theological, moral, and administrative. The communal authority of Paul and his fellow apostles is preeminently epistemological in kind—exercised in theological, spiritual, and moral exposition, instruction, and counseling; but it is significantly political in kind—exercised in giving commands, defining boundaries of belief and conduct, and judging transgressions and offenses. Nevertheless, reflecting the primacy of epistemological authority in their communal service, Paul consistently portrays apostolic leadership and governing as essentially pastoral (shepherding): an expression of fraternal love rather than coercive jurisdiction.[11] In so doing, he raises challenging questions about what distinguishes pastoral authority from coercive jurisdiction and the latter's contribution to the individual and communal life of Christ's faithful people.

Our three postbiblical readings bring substantial theological resources to bear on these questions with diverse results, of interest as much for their wide-ranging and thought-provoking handling of the biblical tradition as for their significant historical influence. In book 19, chapter 14 of his masterpiece of political theology, *The City of God*, completed in 426 CE, Augustine of Hippo shows how the love of God and neighbor available to the faithful believer—in this case, the *pater familias* ruling the household—can transform the institutional arrangements of household governance belonging to our fallen human nature so as to approximate the "natural" familial relationships of responsible, compassionate care for dependent persons ordained by God in creation, prior to his ordination of the punitive and remedial institutions of coercive rule and property (i.e., legal ownership of goods). Key to Augustine's thought in this passage is that the primary relation of equality between the two human objects of divinely commanded love—namely, self and neighbor—requires, first and foremost, that each person takes care of his neighbor's love of God, as of his own; this equality of spiritual care pervades the household relationships of dependence. Importantly, his conception of the transforming power in human relationships of "faith working through love" does not provide a complete earthly resolution of the tension between God's redemption and eschatological perfecting of created human relationships and the persisting destructive dynamics of sinful human orientations and arrangements.

By contrast, Giles of Rome's treatise *On Ecclesiastical Power* provides such an earthly resolution. Giles wrote this tract in 1301 CE as a polemicist for Pope Boniface VIII in his bitter struggle with King Philip IV of France over sovereign jurisdiction of the French church, its clergy, and its property. Giles takes up Augustine's argument that just (righteous) human possession and use of material goods subordinates them to the eschatological end of spiritual perfection, but he converts it into an argument for the pope's universal, jurisdictional sovereignty over rulers, their subjects, and their property.

In making the pope's jurisdictional and proprietary sovereignty indispensable to salvation through the church's action, Giles systematically conflates the spiritual kingdom of Christ imparted by his Spirit through the church's ministry of proclamation (of "word" and "sacrament") and the worldly polity of sinful humanity. By means of a synthesis of neo-Platonic realism and imperial Christology, he portrays the *corpus Christianum* as a seamless spiritual and political/juridical garment: a universal, indivisible, mystical communion and an earthly hierarchy of coercive law and power. The divine-human person of Christ is the celestial head imparting to the body its unity of being, order, and action, while the pope terrestrially mediates the Christological emanation of power and structure to all lesser ranks of agents and authorities. Like the cosmos, Christendom admits no rivalry or tension between distinct orders and rules but only a homogenizing subordination and superordination.

In diametrical opposition to Giles's collapsing of secular and spiritual rule in his ontologizing and positivist account of Christ's earthly *imperium*, the German reformer Martin Luther, in his 1523 tract *Temporal Authority: To What Extent It Should Be Obeyed*, gives expression to the radical tension between Christ's coming kingdom and the passing kingdom of this world. Extrapolating from the apostle Paul's contrast of Christ's rule of his faithful members through the Holy Spirit and God's rule of the Israelite nation through "law" (i.e., temporal judgments, commands, and statutes), Luther argues that Christ's faithful need no worldly regiment of coercive judgment and legal redress since, taught and empowered by the Spirit, they neither commit injustice against others nor seek to avenge injuries against themselves but rather "love everyone" and "suffer injustice and even death willingly." Nevertheless, they uphold secular government out of concern for the weaker neighbor among fellow believers and the common benefit of sinful society, which, being composed primarily of unbelieving evildoers (whatever their outward profession of Christ), needs the law and "the sword" to "preserve peace, punish sin, and restrain the wicked." Luther resolves the practical conflict of not seeking legal protection and redress for oneself while upholding them for all citizens by instructing believers to appeal to the magistrate only on behalf of others so that all may enjoy the goods of public order and justice without making complaints on their own behalf.

Concluding Observation

To recapitulate, the task of my introduction to the collection of Christian texts found in the next chapter has been to explore in a coherent fashion the history of human mediation of God's rule and the ensuing promise and reality of communal identity and action as presented in biblical and postbiblical theological texts. To attempt a summarizing comment is to run the risk of inadequately conveying the rich complexity and dialectical tensions as well as the continuities and discontinuities of this history. Nevertheless, I would venture the following observation: that one major theological challenge for both the Christian church and for Christian secular government throughout their changing historical landscapes has been to determine how much or how little of Israel's communal self-understanding they can and should appropriate, and in what way, within the new parameters given by God's final manifestation of his reign in Jesus Christ. This challenge may resonate at points with the communal challenges faced by Muslims as they strive for an obedient appropriation of their authoritative tradition of divine rule in contemporary cultural and political settings.

Notes

In this essay, all quotations of the Bible are according to the Revised Standard Version.

1. For contemporary scholarship on all the Biblical passages I am introducing, I have found most useful the relevant commentaries in John Barton and John Muddiman, *The Oxford Bible Commentary* (Oxford: Oxford University Press, 2001), hereafter referred to as *OBC*.

2. While there is considerable agreement that, in its agrarian context, debt release is required in the septennial "fallow year," the syntax of verses 2–3 raises further questions regarding, first, the object of the "release": whether it is the debtor, the loan, or even the security or "pledge" taken on the loan from which the creditor is benefiting—possibly a portion of land or its produce, an animal, or implement; and second, the scope of the "release": whether it involves cancellation or deferral of repayment and/or a permanent or temporary return of the security to the debtor. These uncertainties are compounded in the later functioning of the law in urban commercial settings. For a fuller discussion of this debate and the textual ambiguities underlying it, see J. C. McConville, *Deuteronomy*, Apollos Old Testament Commentary 5 (Nottingham: Inter-Varsity Press, 2002), 255–61.

3. For an illuminating exposition of God's gracious judgment of his people in Jesus Christ as their final reconciliation, vindication, and justification, I am indebted to Oliver O'Donovan, *The Desire of the Nations: Rediscovering the Roots of Political Theology* (Cambridge: Cambridge University Press, 1996), 88–146.

4. Eric Franklin, "Luke," in *OBC*, 925.

5. This is C. B. Caird's insight into Luke's understanding of Jesus's teaching of this prayer to his disciples, in *New Testament Theology*, ed. L. D. Hurst (Oxford: Oxford University Press, 1994), 402–3.

6. Loveday Alexander, "Acts," in *OBC*, 1031.

7. In Jesus's post-resurrection commissioning of his disciples in Matthew 28:19, baptismal washing is "in the name of the Father and of the Son and of the Holy Spirit."

8. The complex aspects of this tension are articulated in 1 Cor. 5:6–6:8; and Rom. 12:9–13:10.

9. Deut. 6:4–5: "Hear, O Israel: The Lord our God is one Lord; and you shall love the Lord your God with all your heart, and with all your soul, and with all your might." Lev. 19:17–18: "You shall not hate your brother in your heart, but you shall reason with your neighbor, lest you bear sin because of him. You shall not take vengeance or bear any grudge against the sons of your own people, but you shall love your neighbor as yourself."

10. In Eph. 4:11, the order according to Christ's gifts is "apostles, . . . prophets, . . . evangelists, . . . pastors and teachers." Scholarship overwhelmingly supports the idea that Paul's ordering of services in 1 Cor. 12:28, as in Eph. 4:1, is also a ranking of them, as Anthony C. Thiselton shows in his *The First Epistle to the Corinthians* (Grand Rapids, MI: Eerdmans, 2000), 1013–14.

11. Evidence of the portrayal of apostolic authority as pastoral and fraternal service is in 1 Cor. 4:15–16; 2 Cor. 1:24, 3:4–6; 4:1–2, 11–15; 6:3–13; Gal. 3:24–25; 4:19; 1 Thess. 2:6–7.

Christian Texts on the Community of God's Rule

Deuteronomy 15:1–2, 7–11

God's covenantal law of "release" respecting debt for the Israelites' settled life in the land given by him.

[1]At the end of every seven years you shall grant a release. [2]And this is the manner of the release: every creditor shall release what he has lent to his neighbor; he shall not exact it of his neighbor, his brother, because the Lord's release has been proclaimed. . . . [7]If there is among you a poor man, one of your brethren, in any of your towns within your land which the Lord your God gives you, you shall not harden your heart or shut your hand against your poor brother, [8]but you shall open your hand to him, and lend him sufficient for his need, whatever it may be. [9]Take heed lest there be a base thought in your heart, and you say, "The seventh year, the year of release is near," and your eye be hostile to your poor brother, and you give him nothing, and he cry to the Lord against you, and it be sin in you. [10]You shall give to him freely, and your heart shall not be grudging when you give to him; because for this the Lord your God will bless you in all your work and in all that you undertake. [11]For the poor will never cease out of the land; therefore I command you, You shall open wide your hand to your brother, to the needy and to the poor, in the land.

Matthew 18:15–22

The procedure of fraternal judgment laid down by Jesus the Messiah for his community

[15]"If your brother sins against you, go and tell him his fault, between you and him alone. If he listens to you, you have gained your brother. [16]But if he does not listen, take one or two others along with you, that every word may be confirmed by the evidence of two or three witnesses. [17]If he refuses to listen to them, tell it to the church; and if he refuses to listen even to the church, let him be to you as a Gentile and a tax collector. [18]Truly, I say to you, whatever you bind on earth shall be bound in heaven, and whatever you loose on earth shall be loosed in heaven. [19]Again I say to you, if two of you agree on earth about anything they ask, it will be done for them by my Father in heaven. [20]For where two or three are gathered in my name, there am I in the midst of them." [21]Then Peter came up and said to him, "Lord, how often shall my brother sin against me, and I forgive him? As many as seven times?" [22]Jesus said to him, "I do not say to you seven times, but seventy times seven."

Luke 11:1–4, 9–13

The prayer taught to his disciples by Jesus, imparting sonship of the Father and power of the Holy Spirit

[1]He was praying in a certain place, and when he ceased, one of his disciples said to him, "Lord, teach us to pray, as John taught his disciples." [2]And he said to them, "When you pray, say: "Father, hallowed be thy name. Thy kingdom come. [3]Give us each day our daily bread; [4]and forgive us our sins, for we ourselves forgive every one who is indebted to us; and lead us not into temptation." . . . [9]And I tell you, Ask, and it will be given you; seek, and you will find; knock, and it will be opened to you. [10]For every one who asks receives, and he who seeks finds, and to him who knocks it will be opened. [11]What father among you, if his son asks for a fish, will instead of a fish give him a serpent; [12]or if he asks for an egg, will give him a scorpion? [13]If you then, who are evil, know how to give good gifts to your children, how much more will the heavenly Father give the Holy Spirit to those who ask him!"

Acts 2:36–47

Through the outpouring of the Holy Spirit on the Jewish Day of Pente-
cost, the apostles' testimony to the resurrection and exaltation of Jesus
Christ ushers in the eschatological fellowship of believers and its defining
practices

[36][Peter said:] "Let all the house of Israel therefore know assuredly that God has
made him both Lord and Christ, this Jesus whom you crucified." [37]Now when
they heard this they were cut to the heart, and said to Peter and the rest of the
apostles, "Brethren, what shall we do?" [38]And Peter said to them, "Repent, and
be baptized every one of you in the name of Jesus Christ for the forgiveness of
your sins; and you shall receive the gift of the Holy Spirit. [39]For the promise is to
you and to your children and to all that are far off, every one whom the Lord our
God calls to him." [40]And he testified with many other words and exhorted them,
saying, "Save yourselves from this crooked generation." [41]So those who received
his word were baptized, and there were added that day about three thousand
souls. [42]And they devoted themselves to the apostles' teaching and fellowship, to
the breaking of bread and the prayers.

[43]And fear came upon every soul; and many wonders and signs were done
through the apostles. [44]And all who believed were together and had all things in
common; [45]and they sold their possessions and goods and distributed them to all,
as any had need. [46]And day by day, attending the temple together and breaking
bread in their homes, they partook of food with glad and generous hearts, [47]prais-
ing God and having favor with all the people. And the Lord added to their number
day by day those who were being saved.

Romans 12:9–21

The rich ethos of love among those whose minds are being renewed by the
Spirit of Christ

[9]Let love be genuine; hate what is evil, hold fast to what is good; [10]love one
another with brotherly affection; outdo one another in showing honor. [11]Never
flag in zeal, be aglow with the Spirit, serve the Lord. [12]Rejoice in your hope, be
patient in tribulation, be constant in prayer. [13]Contribute to the needs of the
saints, practice hospitality. [14]Bless those who persecute you; bless and do not
curse them. [15]Rejoice with those who rejoice, weep with those who weep. [16]Live
in harmony with one another; do not be haughty, but associate with the lowly;
never be conceited. [17]Repay no one evil for evil, but take thought for what is
noble in the sight of all. [18]If possible, so far as it depends upon you, live peaceably
with all. [19]Beloved, never avenge yourselves, but leave it to the wrath of God; for
it is written, "Vengeance is mine, I will repay, says the Lord."

[20]No, "if your enemy is hungry, feed him; if he is thirsty, give him drink; for by so doing you will heap burning coals upon his head." [21]Do not be overcome by evil, but overcome evil with good.

1 Corinthians 12:4–7, 28–31

The equality of various and diverse gifts and services within the congregation of Christ's body and their ordering to the common good

[4]Now there are varieties of gifts, but the same Spirit; [5]and there are varieties of service, but the same Lord; [6]and there are varieties of working, but it is the same God who inspires them all in every one. [7]To each is given the manifestation of the Spirit for the common good. . . .
[28]And God has appointed in the church first apostles, second prophets, third teachers, then workers of miracles, then healers, helpers, administrators, speakers in various kinds of tongues. [29]Are all apostles? Are all prophets? Are all teachers? Do all work miracles? [30]Do all possess gifts of healing? Do all speak with tongues? Do all interpret? [31]But earnestly desire the higher gifts.

St. Augustine, *City of God*, book 19, chapter 14 (excerpt)

Outworking of the twofold love command in the Christian household

Divine instruction, furthermore, teaches us two commands above all, the love of God and neighbor. In these there are three objects for our love, God, neighbor and self; but the only safe way of loving self is loving God. From which it follows that we must take care for our neighbor's love of God, in that he or she (wife, children, domestic servants, anyone else) is to be loved as we love ourselves; and, of course, that we desire our neighbor to take care for us, if we need it, in just the same way. By this means we shall live in peace with all men, as far as lies with us; this is *human peace*, a cooperative order of which the principle is that we harm no one and do good to whomever we can.

Our first instinct is for our family, for the arrangements of nature and society itself provide the means and the opportunity to take responsibility. "If any one does not provide for his relatives, and especially for his own family, he has disowned the faith and is worse than an unbeliever." (1 Timothy 5:8). At this point, then, we encounter *domestic peace*, that is to say: "the cooperative order for giving and accepting commands among members of a household." Commands are the business of those who take responsibility, husband for wife, parents for children, masters for servants, and obedience of those for whom responsibility is taken: wives to husbands, children to parents, servants to masters.

But in the household of the just man who lives by faith, those who command really serve. Though they appear to command, their commands do not issue from a craving to dominate, but from a readiness for responsibility, not from a pride that asserts mastery, but from a compassionate care for their material wellbeing. This, of course, is what the arrangements of nature require; it is how God created mankind. "Let him have dominion over the fish of the sea, and over the birds of the air . . . , and over every creeping thing that creeps upon the earth" (Genesis 1:26). The rational creature made in God's image was given dominion over irrational creatures, no more: "not man over man, but man over beast." That is why God made the first righteous men shepherds of flocks, not rulers of men.[1]

Giles of Rome, *On Ecclesiastical Power*, Part 2 (excerpt)

A secular, imperial and absolutist construction of Christ's rule in and through the church

Chapter 8 . . . For the time being, it may be said that he who is not subject to God worthily loses and unjustly possesses all that he holds from God. For the difference between the Eternal King and a temporal king is so great that, if he who is not subject to a temporal king is justly liable to lose all that he holds from that king, it is manifestly clear that he who is not subject to God is still more liable to lose, and more unjust in possessing, that which he holds from God. For if the crime of treason (*lese maiestatis*) renders you worthy of death and unworthy of life and of all your property, then, since majesty (*maiestas*) is an attribute reposed pre-eminently in God, he who is not subject to God is unworthy of himself and of all his possession. And since through original sin we are born not subject to God, and through actual sin we are not subject to Him, then through both kinds of sin we are worthy to lose and unworthily possess all that we hold from God. . . .

Therefore, through the sacrament of baptism, which is the direct remedy against original sin, and through the sacrament of penance, which is the remedy against actual sin, you will be made a worthy lord and a worthy prince and possessor of things. And since these sacraments are not conferred except *in* the Church and *through* the Church, no one is made a worthy lord or a worthy prince or possessor of things except under the Church and through the Church. For no one can receive baptism unless he desires to subject himself to the Church and to be a son of the Church, for the Church is catholic, that is, universal, and there can be no salvation outside her; and no one may receive the sacrament of penance except under the Church and through the Church, for the Lord said to Peter: "Whatever you shall bind", and so on (Matt. 16:19).

Chapter 10 . . . Thus, it will not rest with the bodily physician, but with the spiritual, to judge whether things are possessed justly. Indeed, if due consideration is given to what has been said, (it will be seen that) the earthly power, being royal or imperial power, will have no capacity to judge what is just or unjust except insofar as it does this by virtue of (a delegated) spiritual power. For if justice is a spiritual property and a perfection of soul and not of body, then it will rest with the spiritual power to judge concerning such justice; and earthly and bodily power will have no capacity to judge concerning it unless it does so by virtue of (a delegated) spiritual power. And so all imperial laws and those of the earthly power must be subordinated to the canons of the Church, so that they may derive strength and also firmness from them. Again, all such laws enacted by the earthly power must not contradict the ecclesiastical laws, but must rather be confirmed by the spiritual and ecclesiastical power, so that they may have strength and firmness. For justice is a spiritual property, since it is a kind of rectitude perceptible only to the mind. For we can judge by means of sense what is done or what is not done; but it is with the intellect that we shall judge what is just and what is not just. . . .

If, therefore, the Church is catholic and universal because her lordship is universal, then the faithful are catholic, that is, universal, because they must be universally subject and subservient to the Church. The faithful, then, if they are truly catholic, must be truly subject to the Church universally, so that their manner of possessing themselves and whatever they have is such that they are faithful subjects of the Church in themselves and in all that is theirs. Therefore, from the manner in which things are possessed—since men must hold their possessions as the Church's subjects—(it follows that) the Church will have a universal and total lordship over the possessions of the faithful, but that the lordship which the faithful themselves have will be able to be called (only) particular and partial.[2]

Martin Luther: *Temporal Authority: To What Extent It Should Be Obeyed*

Freedom from, and subjection to, secular authority of the members of Christ's kingdom

Third. Here we must divide the children of Adam and all mankind into two classes, the first belonging to the kingdom of God, the second to the kingdom of the world. Those who belong to the kingdom of God are all the true believers who are in Christ and under Christ, for Christ is King and Lord in the kingdom of God, as Psalm 2:6 and all of Scripture says. . . .

Now observe, these people need no temporal law or sword. If all the world were composed of real Christians, that is, true believers, there would be no need for or benefits from prince, king, lord, sword, or law. They would serve no purpose, since Christians have in their heart the Holy Spirit, who both teaches and makes them to do injustice to no one, to love everyone, and to suffer injustice and even death willingly and cheerfully at the hands of anyone. Where there is nothing but the unadulterated doing of right and bearing of wrong, there is no need for any suit, litigation, court, judge, penalty, law, or sword. For this reason it is impossible that the temporal sword and law should find any work to do among Christians, since they do of their own accord much more than all laws and teachings can demand, just as Paul says in I Timothy 1:9, "The law is not laid down for the just but for the lawless."

Why is this? It is because the righteous man of his own accord does all and more than the law demands. But the unrighteous do nothing that the law demands; therefore, they need the law to instruct, constrain, and compel them to do good. A good tree needs no instruction or law to bear good fruit (cf. Matthew 7:17–18); its nature causes it to bear according to its kind without any law or instruction . . . .

Fifth. But you say: if Christians then do not need the temporal sword or law, why does Paul say to all Christian in Romans 13:1: "Let all souls be subject to the governing authority," and St. Peter: "Be subject to every human ordinance" (1 Peter 2:13), as quoted above? Answer: I have just said that Christians, among themselves and by and for themselves, need no law or sword, since it is neither necessary nor useful for them. Since a true Christian lives and labors on earth not for himself alone but for his neighbor, he does by the very nature of his spirit even what he himself has no need of, but is needful and useful to his neighbor. Because the sword is most beneficial and necessary for the whole world in order to preserve peace, punish sin, and restrain the wicked, the Christian submits most willingly to the rule of the sword, pays his taxes, honors those in authority, serves, helps, and does all he can to assist the governing authority, that it may continue to function and be held in honor and fear. Although he has no need of these things for himself—to him they are not essential—nevertheless, he concerns himself about what is serviceable and of benefit to others, as Paul teaches in Ephesians 5:21–6:9. . . .

From all this we gain the true meaning of Christ's words in Matthew 5:39, "Do not resist evil," etc. It is this: A Christian should be so disposed that he will suffer every evil and injustice without avenging himself; neither will he seek legal redress in the courts but have utterly no need of temporal authority and law for his own sake. On behalf of others, however, he may and should seek vengeance, justice, protection, and help, and do as much as he can to achieve it. Likewise, the governing authority should, on its own initiative or through the instigation of others, help and protect him too, without any complaint, application, or instigation on his own part. If it fails to do this, he should permit himself to be despoiled and slandered; he should not resist evil, as Christ's words say.[3]

Notes

In this chapter, all biblical passages are according to the Revised Standard Version (National Council of Churches of Christ, 1951).

1. Translation by Oliver O'Donovan, in Oliver O'Donovan and Joan Lockwood O'Donovan, eds., *From Irenaeus to Grotius: A Sourcebook in Christian Political Thought* (Grand Rapids, MI: Eerdmans, 1999), 157. Reprinted with permission of the publisher.

2. From R. W. Dyson, trans., *Giles of Rome's* On Ecclesiastical Power: *A Medieval Theory of World Government* (New York: Columbia University Press, 2004), 173, 175, 181. Reprinted with permission of the publisher.

3. From Martin Luther, *Temporal Authority: To What Extent It Should Be Obeyed*, trans. J. J. Schindel, rev. W. I. Brandt, *Luther's Works*, vol. 45 (Philadelphia: Fortress, 1962). Reprinted with permission of the publisher.

PART FOUR

Political Power and Faith

The Role of the Community in the Broader World

Islamic Perspectives

MAHAN MIRZA

"Muslims are assured in the Qur'an," writes the historian Marshall Hodgson, "'You have become the best community ever raised up for mankind, enjoining the right and forbidding the wrong, and having faith in God' . . . . Earnest men have taken this prophecy seriously to the point of trying to mold the history of the whole world in accordance with it."[1] The *Venture of Islam*—the title of Hodgson's three-volume work—is a venture that interrupts history with divine command. The Indian poet philosopher Muhammad Iqbal (d. 1938) echoes this "Islamic vision in religion and civilization" by contrasting prophetic consciousness with that of the mere mystic. The end for the mystic is union or annihilation with the divine. But what the mystic aspires for as an "end" is for the prophet just the beginning. The prophet is both *'abd*, a slave who turns his face to God, and *rasūl*, an emissary commissioned to translate his spiritual communion with God into a force of history.[2] In doing so, the prophet partners with a community of believers. With these thoughts from Hodgson and Iqbal in mind, I selected texts from the Islamic tradition that could stimulate a discussion of the role of the community in the broader world, grouping these selections under four headings: manifest destiny, striving in God's path, citizenship and alliances, and social responsibility. These texts can be found in the chapter following this essay.

The texts I have placed under the heading of "Manifest Destiny" speak to the imperative of *iqāmat al-dīn* or "establishing the *dīn*." *Dīn* is a word that is loosely translated as "religion"; in the term *iqāmat al-dīn,* it is compounded with the same imperative that commands believers to "establish" the ritual prayer. In this vein, I invite the reader to think about what the term *aqīmū-'l-dīn* (establish the religion[3]) means in Q. 42:13.[4]

In Sura 5:44–48, the Qur'an speaks about the need to "judge by that which God has revealed" (*ḥukm bi-mā anzala Allāh*). Addressing the three Abrahamic traditions in succession, the verses remind believers that in revelation is "guidance and light," and that those who judge by other than what God has revealed are transgressors. What does "judging by that which God has revealed" mean in today's world? How would these texts operate in cosmopolitan societies with secular polities? Do these verses apply in contexts where religion is purely a private affair and a matter of personal conscience? Qur'anic verses 4:75 and 57:25 elaborate that the purpose of God's guidance and laws is not merely for God's glory but to liberate the oppressed and to establish justice on earth.

This idea of justice is linked to the notion of "mean" or "balance." It evokes a state of being between extremes, as used in virtue ethics, a system inherited from classical philosophy that was incorporated into Muslim thought. It is also at the heart of what it means to be a community or *umma*—a just or "middle" community—constituted primarily so that believers may bear witness to the rest of humanity (Q. 2:143). Indeed, is it not God's promise that as long as believers stay true to God's covenant, they will inherit the earth (Q. 24:55)? The prophecy that Islam will spread to the entire world is echoed in numerous prophetic reports (hadiths), some of which have been chosen for our reading and reflection in this seminar.

The second group of texts moves from "manifest destiny" to *jihād fī sabīl Allāh*: an all-out struggle in the path of God. According to these texts, the goal to bear witness and establish justice through God's divine command will not be achieved by sitting idly by, lost in daily devotions. It requires commitment and sacrifice. Jihad is not merely a matter of self-defense or some kind of internal struggle against one's inner demons. It also applies to both an individual and collective struggle to stand as witnesses before all of humanity, to make the word of God supreme (Q. 22:78 and 61:9–10).

But one should not lose sight of the ultimate goal, which is the earning of God's pleasure and everlasting life in gardens of bliss, over and above any secular aim of worldly success or domination, although that may also be awarded in the process as a fringe benefit (Q. 61:12–13). Believers should be mindful, however, that there are rules even to armed conflict (Q. 2:190–91 and 22:39–41) and that knowledge can be a double-edged sword. They must use knowledge to elevate God's word and establish His *dīn*, not for worldly gain and riches by interpreting scripture to please people and maintain authority over them (Q. 9:33–34). Scholars, as one prophetic report reminds us, are the true heirs to the prophets.

In the third collection of texts, our attention turns to the question of alliances and membership in the prophetic community of believers. As long as the struggle between the forces of faith and disbelief is active, the believers must never allow the line to be blurred between friend and foe (Q. 48:29). However, those who are not part of the community of believers but have not stood in the way of the divine mission may be dealt with kindly and justly (Q. 60:8–9).

As "people of the book," Jews and Christians have special standing, but they are to remain outsiders. They should not be fully integrated as partners or members of the community of believers (Q. 5:51 and 9:29). "Polytheists," on the other hand, who ascribe partners to God, are altogether unclean and to be anathematized (Q. 9:28). How could it be otherwise when God has written: "I most certainly shall triumph, I and My messengers" (Q. 58:21). Those who oppose God and His messenger are the party of Satan (*hizb al-shaytān*), while those who are with God and His messenger are the party of God (*hizb Allāh*) (Q. 58:19–22).

That the power of God merges with the power of the prophet and the believers as a vital force in history is undeniable on a plain-sense reading of Muslim scripture. In texts that could not be included in our reading for this seminar, we are told that on one occasion, when the believers pledged themselves in allegiance to the messenger under a tree at a time of great crisis, "The hand of God was above their hands" (Q. 48:10); in battle when the prophet threw sand to blind the enemy, or when the enemies of God fell on the field, the Qur'an proclaims, "It was not you who slew them; rather, God slew them. And it was not you who threw when you threw; rather, it was God who threw" (Q. 8:17); "If you help God, He will help you" (Q. 47:7). As agents moving through history with divine authority and force, the messenger and community of believers are intimately entangled, even to the point of participation in God's honor: "And to God belongs [all] honor, and to His messenger, and to the believers, but the hypocrites do not know" (Q. 63:8).

The vision we get from these texts with the accent, emphasis, and arrangement presented here has been articulated by Islamists such as Abu'l A'la Mawdudi (d. 1979), as apparent in his interpretation of Q. 9:29.[5] Alternative visions of Islam that are more inclusive and in step with the concept of cosmopolitan and liberal citizenship are also possible, but in order to bring them to light, we would require a different selection of texts. One such attempt has been articulated by traditional scholars with the support of Muslim leaders such King Mohammad VI of Morocco in the recent Marrakesh Declaration, in partnership with Shaikh Abdallah Bin Bayyah's Forum for Promoting Peace.[6] In that declaration, scholars of traditional Islam from around the world use a host of interpretive strategies to contextualize and interpret verses from the Qur'an and prophetic reports to establish the imperative of equal citizenship of minorities in Muslim societies as being the true representation of God's will. The declaration draws in particular on the Constitution of Medina, reading it in light of "the higher purposes of God's law" or *maqāsid al-sharī'a*, to call for a vision of Muslim societies that respects freedom of religion, pluralism, and equality before the law for all citizens.

This brings me to the fourth group of selected texts, those focusing on social responsibility. How are everyday believers supposed to think about power when they are largely powerless? One way, according to the Qur'an, is to be patient and to persevere (Q. 103), another is to keep participating in generosity through small acts of neighborly kindness (Q. 107), and a third way is to simply take solace in prayer and supplication, directing one's appeals against tyrants straight to God (Q. 58:1).

Prophetic reports offer additional ways to cope: one course of action may be to withdraw altogether from society into the wilderness. Certain prophetic reports on nonviolence provide a stark contrast to other reports or verses of the Qur'an that call for retaliation, apparently contradicting some historical examples from the prophet Muhammad's life and career in which he engaged in armed conflict. One of the reasons why competing visions of Islam can live side-by-side is precisely this: that one part of Muhammad's life seems to be very different from another part of his life. There are many strategies that traditional Muslim scholarship adopted in order to make sense of texts that seem to be providing conflicting guidance.

One of the most prominent ways in which apparent contradictions in the texts are reconciled is by contextualizing them within different periods of the prophet Muhammad's life. Verses and prophetic sayings that exhort to nonviolence and forgiveness are invariably placed in Mecca, the first part of Muhammad's prophetic career, when he was powerless. The selections from section 4 of the next chapter are examples from that period. The texts chosen for the first three sections are, however, from Medina, when the Muslim community was better established and able to exercise a degree of coercion that was not possible earlier.

The celebrated scholar of Islam William Montgomery Watt captures the contrasting two periods in Muhammad's life in a clever title to the messenger's succinct biography: *Muhammad: Prophet and Statesman.*[7] According to Watt, Muhammad's life in Mecca was similar to that of prophets in the Western imagination: persecuted, nonviolent, with a small band of ragged followers. In Medina, however, the tables turn, and Muhammad's life resembles that of a statesman: political leader, master strategist, visionary negotiator, general in arms.

Watt's thesis is presented more elaborately in his two-volume study on Muhammad's life: the first titled *Muhammad at Mecca* and the second *Muhammad at Medina.*[8] In contrasting these two periods of Muhammad's life, Watt accentuates and repurposes categories that Muslim scholars had themselves known and established since the earliest times. But there are many ways in which the shift from Mecca to Medina can be read. The predominant way of reading the contrast is through the lens of abrogation. In such a reading, Muhammad's role as God's emissary remains constant; he is nonviolent and appeasing when acting in a personal capacity or when it is strategically advantageous. But when in a position of strength, he is able to enter the arena of statecraft, diplomacy, and warfare. According to this line of interpretation, God sent instructions to Muhammad appropriate to the time and circumstance; however, all things being equal, what comes later generally abrogates and annuls what came earlier.

This manner of reading—through the lens of abrogation—has the potential of carrying with it some very negative implications. Among these are that Muslims can be nonviolent, inclusive, and tolerant when weak for the purpose of gaining strategic advantages that, once gained, will enable them to apply different standards after they have come to power. An example of this kind of reading comes through the interpretation of verses such as Q. 9:60 in which alms may be given to non-Muslims whose "hearts are to be reconciled." At least one opinion, based on a saying of the second Caliph ʿUmar and adopted by the earliest Sunni legal school—that of Abu Hanifa—maintains the following opinion, as recorded by Mawdudi: "When the number and power of Muslims increased . . . they no longer stood in need of any support from such people."[9]

Another approach adopted by some scholars in the latter part of the twentieth century flips the script by suggesting that the Meccan context is the expression of God's will in universal terms, while the Medinan context is the application of universal principles to a specific historical moment. This approach has been adopted by Mahmoud Mohamed Taha (d. 1985) in his *Second Message of Islam*, and it is echoed in the writings of prominent and influential scholars like Fazlur Rahman (d. 1988).[10] These meta-lenses come together with a variety of sophisticated hermeneutic tools on textual interpretation to form a rich and complex tradition of Islamic scholarship.[11] Close reading and discussion can draw on this rich tradition to complicate the relatively straightforward story of manifest destiny and jihad that is set up in the selection of texts found in the chapter following this essay.

Among the tools that interpreters draw on are legal and ethical maxims (*qawāʿid*) embedded in tradition and culture, a few of which have been selected to complete the selection of texts for this section. Maxims help to set the priorities and moral compass of both those in power and those vying for it. Some maxims are based on ethical principles; others are simply pragmatic: tyranny is better than anarchy; whose power is established, obedience to him is incumbent; harm must be eliminated; custom is the basis of judgment. Each of these provides a clue into the reasoning of scholars, jurists, citizens, and leaders.

In conclusion, let me say that I have chosen the texts found in the next chapter and put together this narrative as a provocation. In preparation for the Building Bridges Seminar 2017, we were invited to select material from what may be considered the "too difficult" tray: texts that make us uncomfortable, texts that draw on popular narratives and conceptions of our traditions that need to be engaged systematically and deeply in settings that facilitate dialogical intertextual study. I accepted that invitation, convinced that the seminar's trust and fellowship inspire confidence that we are not building bridges to nowhere.

Notes

1. Marshall Hodgson, *Venture of Islam: Conscience and History in a World Civilization* (Chicago: University of Chicago Press, 1974), 1:71. Citations omitted.

2. See Muhammad Iqbal, "Lecture V: The Spirit of Muslim Culture," in *The Reconstruction of Religious Thought in Islam*, 99–115 (Stanford, CA: Stanford University Press, 2012).

3. Abdel Haleem renders the term "uphold the faith." See M. A. S. Abdel Haleem, trans., *The Qur'an: English Translation and Parallel Arabic Text* (New York: Oxford University Press, 2010), 484.

4. In this essay, passages from the Qur'an are the author's own or are according to Mohammed Marmaduke Pickthall, *The Meaning of the Glorious Qur'ān* (Hyderabad-Deccan: Government Central Press, 1930), modified slightly.

5. See Sayyid Abul A'lā Mawdūdī, *Towards Understanding the Qur'ān*, vol. 3, surahs 7–9 (Leicester: Islamic Foundation, 1990), 202.

6. *The Marrakesh Declaration on the Rights of Religious Minorities in Predominantly Muslim Majority Communities* was the outcome of a summit, January 25–27, 2016, organized by His Majesty King Mohammed VI in conjunction with the Forum for Promoting Peace in Muslim Societies.

7. W. M. Watt, *Muhammad: Prophet and Statesman* (Oxford: Oxford University Press, 1974).

8. W. M. Watt, *Muhammad at Mecca* (Oxford: Oxford University Press, 1953); and W. M. Watt, *Muhammad at Medina* (Oxford: Oxford University Press, 1956).

9. Mawdudi, *Tafhīm al-Qur'ān*, 9:60, trans. http://englishtafsir.com/Quran/9/index .html#sdfootnote65sym, accessed June 1, 2019.

10. Mahmoud Mohamed Taha, *The Second Message of Islam*, rev. ed. (Syracuse: Syracuse University Press, 1996); and Fazlur Rahman, *Islam and Modernity: Transformation of an Intellectual Tradition* (Chicago: University of Chicago Press, 1982).

11. An accessible resource for hermeneutic tools in the Islamic tradition is Mohammad Hashim Kamali, *Principles of Islamic Jurisprudence*, rev. ed. (Cambridge: Islamic Texts Society, 2005).

Islamic Texts for Dialogue on Community in the Broader World

Manifest Destiny

This section presents texts that speak about the spread of Islam to the entire world. The idea of *iqāmat al-dīn* (establishing [or "upholding"] the religion) (42:13) is central to the ambitions of political Islamic movements. The twin purposes of *iqāmat al-dīn* would be to live by the laws of God (*ḥukm bi-mā anzala Allāh*) (5:44–48) and to spread the light of God to all of humanity (2:143) by liberating people from oppression (4:75) and establishing justice, which has been the mission of all the prophets and revealed scriptures (57:25). As long as believers are sincere and do their best, they will inherit the earth (24:55).

Surat al-Shura [42]:13

He has ordained for you the same religion that He commended to Noah, and that which We reveal to you (Muhammad), and that We commended to Abraham and Moses and Jesus, saying: Establish the religion, and be not divided therein. Dreadful for the idolaters is that unto which you call them. God chooses for Himself whom He please, and guides to Himself whomever turns (toward Him).

Surat al-Ma'ida [5]:44–48

[44]We revealed the Torah, wherein is guidance and a light, by which the prophets who surrendered (to God) judged the Jews; and the rabbis and the priests (judged) by such of God's Scripture as they were bidden to preserve, and unto which they were witnesses. So, do not fear humankind, but fear Me. And do not sell My revelations for a puny sum. Whosoever judges not by that which God has revealed: such are disbelievers. [45]And We prescribed for them therein: The life

for the life, and the eye for the eye, and the nose for the nose, and the ear for the ear, and the tooth for the tooth, and for wounds an equivalent wound. But whosoever forgoes it (out of charity), it shall be expiation for him. Whosoever judges not by that which God has revealed: such are wrong-doers. [46]And We caused Jesus, son of Mary, to follow in their footsteps, confirming that which was (revealed) before him in the Torah; and We bestowed on him the Gospel wherein is guidance and a light, confirming that which was (revealed) before it in the Torah—a guidance and an admonition to those who take heed. [47]Let the People of the Gospel judge by that which God has revealed therein. Whosoever judges not by that which Allah hath revealed: such are iniquitous. [48]And to you have We revealed the Scripture with the truth, confirming whatever Scripture was before it, and a guardian over it. So judge between them by that which God has revealed, and follow not their desires away from the truth which has come to you. For each We have appointed a divine law and a traced-out way. Had God willed He could have made you one community. But that He may try you by that which He has given you (He has made you as you are). So vie one with another in good works. To God you will all return, and He will then inform you of that wherein you differ.

Surat al-Nisa' [4]:75

Why should you not fight for the cause of God and of the feeble among men, women, and children who are crying, "Our Lord! Bring us forth from out this town whose people are oppressors! Oh, give us from a protector! Give us from a defender!"?

Surat al-Hadid [57]:25

We sent Our messengers with clear proofs, and revealed with them the Scripture and the Balance, so that humankind may observe justice; and He revealed iron, wherein is mighty power and (many) uses for humankind, so that God may know those who help Him and His messengers, though (God remains) unseen. Indeed, God is Strong, Almighty.

Surat al-Baqara [2]:143

We have appointed you [believers to be] a middle community, so that you may bear witness to humankind and so that the Messenger may bear witness to you.

Surat al-Nur [24]:55

God has promised such of you as believe and do good work that He will surely make them vicegerents on the earth even as He caused those who were before them to be vicegerents; and that He will surely establish for them the religion that He has approved for them and will give them security in exchange for their fear. They serve Me. They ascribe no thing as partner unto Me. Those who disbelieve henceforth, they are the evildoers.

Hadith

Musnad Ahmad ibn Hanbal 18596[1]

Narrated by Hudhayfa b. Yaman who said: "The messenger of God said: 'Prophethood will remain among you for as long as God wills. He then will terminate it when He wills. Then there will be the Caliphate on the prophethood paradigm. It will remain for as long as God wills. He will then terminate it when He wills. Then there will be harsh monarchy. It will remain for as long as God wills. He then will eliminate it when He wills. Then there will be oppressive monarchy. It will remain for as long as God wills. He then will eliminate it when He wills. Then there will be the Caliphate on the prophethood paradigm.' And then he was silent."

Sunan al-Tirmidhi 2176[2]

On the authority of Thawban, who said: "The messenger of God (may the peace and blessings of God be upon him) said: 'God contracted the earth for me. I saw its easts and wests. The dominion of my community (*umma*) will reach all over that which was contracted for me.'"

Musnad Ahmad ibn Hanbal 23879[3]

Miqdad ibn Aswad said: "I heard the messenger of God (may God be pleased with him) say: 'There will not remain on the face of the earth a house—neither established nor mobile—save that God will insert into it the word of submission, honoring the worthy or humbling the humble. If God honors them, He will make them worthy of it. If He humbles them, they will be its subjects.'"

Sahih Muslim 126:34[4]

On the authority of Abu Hurayra is that the messenger of God said: "I have been commanded to fight people until they testify that there is no god but God, and they believe in me along with that which I have brought. If they were to do that, their blood and wealth is safe from me, except for what may be rightfully claimed. And it is for God to take them to account."

Hadith al-Suyuti 129[5]

The Messenger of God said: "If you pass a zone without a governor (*sultan*), do not enter it, for the governor is the shadow (*zill*) of God and his the spear (*rumh*) on earth. . . . Whosoever honors him is honored by God, and whosoever scorns him is scorned by God."

Striving in God's Path

Iqāmat al-dīn requires striving in the path of God (22:78 and 61:9–13) while being cautious of a professional religious class (scholars/priests/rabbis) who speak in God's name but work for their own interests (9:33–34). But striving should also be within limits (2:190–91) and in self-defense (22:39–41).

Surat al-Hajj [22]:78

Strive for God with the endeavor which is His right. He has chosen you and has not placed upon you in religion any hardship; the faith of your father Abraham (is yours). He has named you *muslims* (both) in times past and in this (Scripture), that the messenger may bear witness to you, and that you may bear witness to humankind. So establish worship, pay the alms, and hold fast to God. He is your Protector. A blessed Patron and a blessed Helper!

Surat al-Saff [61]:9–13

⁹He it is Who has sent His messenger with guidance and the religion of truth, that He may make it prevail over all religion, however much idolaters may be averse. ¹⁰O you who believe! Shall I show you a commerce that will save you from a painful doom? ¹¹You should believe in God and His messenger, and should strive for the cause of God with your wealth and your lives. That is better for you, if you did but know. ¹²He will forgive your sins and bring you into Gardens underneath which rivers flow, into pleasant dwellings in Gardens of Eden. That is the supreme triumph. ¹³And (He will give you) something else that you will love: help from God and present victory. Give good tidings (O Muhammad) to believers.

Surat al-Tawba [9]:33–34

³³He it is Who has sent His messenger with guidance and the religion of truth, that He may cause it to prevail over all religion, however much the idolaters may be averse. ³⁴O ye who believe! Many rabbis and monks devour people's wealth of humankind wantonly and debar people from God's path. To those who hoard gold and silver and spend it not on the cause of God, give them give (O Muhammad) of a painful doom.

Surat al-Baqara [2]:190–91

[190]Fight in the way of God against those who fight against you, but do not begin hostilities. Truly, God does not love aggressors. [191]And slay them wherever you find them, and drive them out of the places from which they drove you out, for persecution is worse than slaughter. And do not fight with them at the Sacred Mosque unless they first attack you there; but if they do attack you (there), then slay them. Such is the reward of disbelievers.

Surat al-Hajj [22]:39–41

[39]Permission is given unto those who fight because they have been wronged; and God is indeed able to give them victory—[40]those who have been driven from their homes unjustly only because they said, "Our Lord is God." For had it not been for God's repelling some people by means of others, [then many] cloisters and churches and synagogues and mosques, wherein the Name of God is often mentioned, would assuredly have been destroyed. Indeed, God helps those who help Him—truly, God is Strong, Almighty—[41]those who, if We give them power in the land, establish worship and pay the alms tax and enjoin kindness and forbid iniquity. And God's is the outcome of events.

Hadith

Sunan al-Tirmidhi 2682[6]

Abu al-Darda' is reported to have said that he heard the messenger of God (may God's peace and blessings be upon him), say: "Scholars are the inheritors of prophets. Prophets do not bequeath wealth (*dīnars* and *dirhams*). They bequeath knowledge."

Citizenship and Alliances

Believers must band together with each other, but they are free to make alliances with those who do not resist their mission (Q. 48:29; Q. 60:8–9). They should beware of taking Jews and Christians as protecting friends (Q. 5:51). Pagans may not be considered citizens; others with questionable beliefs may be tolerated in exchange for a special tax (Q. 9:28–29). The prophetic struggle is ultimately a cosmic conflict between the party of God (*ḥizb Allāh*) and the party of Satan (Q. 58:19–22).

Surat al-Fath [48]:29

Muhammad is the messenger of God. And those who are with him are harsh against the disbelievers and merciful among themselves. You see them bowing and prostrating (in worship), seeking bounty from God and contentment. The mark on their foreheads is from the traces of prostration. Such is their likeness in the Torah and their likeness in the Gospel—like as sown corn that sends forth its shoot and strengthens it and rises firm upon its stalk, delighting the sowers—that He may enrage the disbelievers with them. God has promised forgiveness and immense reward to those who believe and do good works.

Surat al-Mumtahana [60]:8-9

[8]He does not forbid you to deal kindly and justly with anyone who has not fought you for your faith or driven you out of your homes: God loves the just. [9]But God forbids you to take as allies those who have fought against you for your faith, driven you out of your homes, and helped others to drive you out: any of you who take them as allies will truly be wrongdoers.

Surat al-Ma'ida [5]:51

O ye who believe! Do not take Jews and Christians for allies. They are allies to one another. Anyone among you who takes them for allies is (one) of them. Truly, God does not guide such wrongdoing folk.

Surat al-Tawba [9]:28-29

[28]O ye who believe! The idolaters surely are unclean. So do not let them come near the Sacred Mosque after this, their year. If you fear poverty (from the loss of their merchandise), [keep in mind that] God shall preserve you out of His bounty if He wishes. Indeed, God is Knower, Wise. [29]Fight against such of those who have been given the Scripture yet do not believe in God nor the Last Day, and do not forbid that which God and His Messenger have forbidden, and do not follow the Religion of Truth—until they pay the tribute readily, being humbled.

Surat al-Mujadila [58]:19-22

[19]Satan has gained control over them and made them forget God. They are on Satan's side, and Satan's side will be the losers: [20]those who oppose God and His Messenger will be among the most humiliated. [21]God has written, "I shall most certainly win, I and My messengers." God is powerful and almighty. [22][Prophet], you will not find people who truly believe in God and the Last Day giving their loyalty to those who oppose God and His Messenger, even though they may be their fathers, sons, brothers, or other relations: these are the people in whose hearts God has inscribed faith, and whom He has strengthened with His spirit.

He will let them enter Gardens graced with flowing streams, where they will stay: God is well pleased with them, and they with Him. They are on God's side, and God's side will be the one to prosper.

Mawdudi on Surat al-Tawba [9]:29[7]

Here Sayyid Abul A'lā Mawdudi (1903–1979) comments on Q. 9:29: "Those who do not believe in God and the Last Day—even though they were given the scriptures, and who do not hold as unlawful that which God and His Messenger have declared to be unlawful, and who do not follow the true religion—fight against them until they pay tribute out of their hand and are utterly subdued."

The purpose for which the Muslims are required to fight is not as one might think to compel the unbelievers into embracing Islam. Rather, their purpose is to put an end to the sovereignty and supremacy of the unbelievers so that the latter are unable to rule over men. The authority to rule should only be vested in those who follow the true faith; unbelievers who do not follow this true faith should live in a state of subordination. Unbelievers are required to pay *jizyah* (poll tax) in lieu of the security provided to them as the Dhimmis ("Protected People") of an Islamic state. *Jizyah* symbolizes the submission of the unbelievers to the suzerainty of Islam. "To pay *jizyah* of their own hands humbled" refers to payment in a state of submission. "Humbled" also reinforces the idea that the believers, rather than the unbelievers, should be the rulers in performance of their duty as God's vicegerents. . . .

Some nineteenth-century Muslim writers and their followers in our own times never seem to tire of their apologies for *jizyah*. But God's religion does not require that apologetic explanations be made on its behalf. The simple fact is that according to Islam, non-Muslims have been granted the freedom to stay outside the Islamic fold and to cling to their false, man-made, ways if they so wish. They have, however, absolutely no right to seize the reins of power in any part of God's earth nor to direct the collective affairs of human beings according to their own misconceived doctrines. For if they are given such an opportunity, corruption and mischief will ensue. In such a situation the believers would be under an obligation to do their utmost to dislodge them from political power and to make them live in subservience to the Islamic way of life.

The Marrakesh Declaration

The Marrakesh Declaration on the Rights of Religious Minorities in Predominantly Muslim Majority Communities was the outcome of a summit, January 25–27, 2016, organized by His Majesty King Mohammed VI in conjunction with the Forum for Promoting Peace in Muslim Societies. It makes eight key points, each supported by the Qur'an:

1. God bestowed dignity to all human beings regardless of their race, color, language, or belief, for God breathed His spirit into their forefather Adam, upon him be peace. [Q. 17:70]
2. This dignity requires that humans are granted freedom of choice. [Q. 2:256, 10:99]
3. All people—regardless of their different natures, societies, and worldviews—share the bonds of brotherhood and sisterhood in humanity. [Q. 49:13]
4. God established the heavens and the earth on the basis of justice and made such justice the standard for all human interaction in order to ward off resentment and enmity, and He encouraged benevolence between people in order to nurture love and harmony. [Q. 16:90]
5. Peace is the hallmark of Islam and the primary purpose of Sacred Law for society. [Q. 2:208, 8:61]
6. God Almighty sent Prophet Muhammad, upon him peace and blessings, as a mercy to the worlds. [Q. 21:107]
7. Islam calls for treating others kindly, regardless of whether they share the same beliefs or not. [Q. 60:8]
8. Islamic Sacred Law strongly emphasizes honoring contracts, covenants, and conventions that ensure peace and coexistence between peoples. [Q. 5:1, 16:91]

Here follows the official executive summary of the declaration:[8]

In the Name of God, the All-Merciful, the All-Compassionate

WHEREAS, conditions in various parts of the Muslim World have deteriorated dangerously due to the use of violence and armed struggle as a tool for settling conflicts and imposing one's point of view;

WHEREAS, this situation has also weakened the authority of legitimate governments and enabled criminal groups to issue edicts attributed to Islam, but which, in fact, alarmingly distort its fundamental principles and goals in ways that have seriously harmed the population as a whole;

WHEREAS, this year marks the 1,400th anniversary of the Charter of Medina, a constitutional contract between the Prophet Muhammad, God's peace and blessings be upon him, and the people of Medina, which guaranteed the religious liberty of all, regardless of faith;

WHEREAS, hundreds of Muslim scholars and intellectuals from over 120 countries, along with representatives of Islamic and international organizations, as well as leaders from diverse religious groups and nationalities, gathered in Marrakesh on this date to reaffirm the principles of the Charter of Medina at a major conference;

WHEREAS, this conference was held under the auspices of His Majesty, King Mohammed VI of Morocco, and organized jointly by the Ministry of Endowment and Islamic Affairs in the Kingdom of Morocco and the Forum for Promoting Peace in Muslim Societies based in the United Arab Emirates;

AND NOTING the gravity of this situation afflicting Muslims as well as peoples of other faiths throughout the world, and after thorough deliberation and discussion, the convened Muslim scholars and intellectuals:

DECLARE HEREBY our firm commitment to the principles articulated in the Charter of Medina, whose provisions contained a number of the principles of constitutional contractual citizenship, such as freedom of movement, property ownership, mutual solidarity and defense, as well as principles of justice and equality before the law; and that,

The objectives of the Charter of Medina provide a suitable framework for national constitutions in countries with Muslim majorities, and the United Nations Charter and related documents, such as the Universal Declaration of Human Rights, are in harmony with the Charter of Medina, including consideration for public order.

NOTING FURTHER that deep reflection upon the various crises afflicting humanity underscores the inevitable and urgent need for cooperation among all religious groups, we

AFFIRM HEREBY that such cooperation must be based on a "Common Word," requiring that such cooperation must go beyond mutual tolerance and respect, to providing full protection for the rights and liberties to all religious groups in a civilized manner that eschews coercion, bias, and arrogance.

BASED ON ALL OF THE ABOVE, we hereby:

Call upon Muslim scholars and intellectuals around the world to develop a jurisprudence of the concept of "citizenship" which is inclusive of diverse groups. Such jurisprudence shall be rooted in Islamic tradition and principles and mindful of global changes.

Urge Muslim educational institutions and authorities to conduct a courageous review of educational curricula that addresses honestly and effectively any material that instigates aggression and extremism, leads to war and chaos, and results in the destruction of our shared societies;

Call upon politicians and decision makers to take the political and legal steps necessary to establish a constitutional contractual relationship among its citizens, and to support all formulations and initiatives that aim to fortify relations and understanding among the various religious groups in the Muslim World;

Call upon the educated, artistic, and creative members of our societies, as well as organizations of civil society, to establish a broad movement for the just treatment of religious minorities in Muslim countries and to raise awareness as to their rights, and to work together to ensure the success of these efforts.

Call upon the various religious groups bound by the same national fabric to address their mutual state of selective amnesia that blocks memories of centuries of joint and shared living on the same land; we call upon them to rebuild the past by reviving this tradition of conviviality, and restoring our shared trust that has been eroded by extremists using acts of terror and aggression;

Call upon representatives of the various religions, sects and denominations to confront all forms of religious bigotry, vilification, and denigration of what people hold sacred, as well as all speech that promote hatred and bigotry; AND FINALLY,

AFFIRM that it is unconscionable to employ religion for the purpose of aggressing upon the rights of religious minorities in Muslim countries.

Marrakesh
January 2016, 27th

Social Responsibility

This section lays out texts that speak of the need for Muslims to be socially responsible, if not politically engaged. Sometimes, prayer is the only recourse for the powerless. There may also be times when it is better to withdraw entirely.

Surat al-Asr [103]

In the name of God, the Compassionate, the Merciful
[1]By the declining day, [2]truly, humankind is in loss, [3]except for those who believe and do good deeds, exhort one another to truth, and exhort one another to patience.

Surat al-Maʿun [107]

In the name of God, the Compassionate, the Merciful

[1]Have you observed the one who belies religion? [2]That is the one who repels the orphan, [3]and does not urge the feeding of the needy. [4]Ah, woe to worshippers [5]who are heedless of their prayer; [6]who would be seen (at worship) [7]yet refuse small kindnesses!

Surat al-Mujadila [58]:1

God has heard the words of her that disputes with you (Muhammad) concerning her husband and complains to God. And God hears your conversation. Indeed, God is Hearer, Knower.

Hadith

Sunan Abu Daʾud 4031[9]

Ibn ʿUmar said that the messenger of God (may God's peace and blessings be upon him) said: "Whoever imitates a people is from among them."

Sahih al-Bukhari 13[10]

On the authority of Anas that the messenger of God (may God's peace and blessings be upon him) said: "None of you truly believes until he loves for his brother what he loves for himself."

Sunan Abu Daʾud 4344[11]

On the authority of Abu Saʿid al-Khudhri who said: "The messenger of God (may God's peace and blessings be upon him) said: 'The best jihad is a just word spoken before an oppressive ruler.'"

Sahih Muslim [177] 78[12]

Abu Saʿid said: "I heard the messenger of God (may God be pleased with him) say: 'If anyone from among you were to witness something wrong, he should change it with his hand (by acting); if he is unable to do so, then (he should change it) with his tongue (by speaking out); if he is unable to do so (by either of these means), then (he should change it by not accepting it) in his heart. And that is the weakest state of faith.'"

Sunan al-Tirmidhi 2194[13]

Saʿd b. Abi Waqqas is reported to have said at the time of the civil strife during the reign of ʿUthman b. ʿAffan: "I bear witness that the messenger of God (May God's peace and blessings be upon him) said: 'There is a tribulation to come in which the one who sits will be better than the one standing; the one standing better than the one who walks; the one who walks better than the one who runs.'"

He [Sa'd] asked: "What do you say if someone enters my home and stretches out his hand to take my life?" He [the prophet] replied: "Be like the son of Adam."

Sahih Muslim [196] 95[14]

On the authority of Tamim al-Dari that the prophet (may God's peace and blessings be upon him) said: "Religion (*al-dīn*) is sincerity (or good counsel, *al-naṣīḥa*)." We [the companions who were present] asked: "To whom?" He replied: "To God, His book, His messenger, the leaders of the Muslim community, and the general body of believers."

Well-Known Political, Ethical, and Legal Maxims

- Tyranny is better than anarchy.
- Whose power is established, obedience to him is incumbent.
- Harm must be eliminated.
- Custom is the basis of judgment.

Notes

In this chapter, Qur'an verses are according to Mohammed Marmaduke Pickthall, *The Meaning of the Glorious Qur'ān* (1930), adapted slightly. All hadiths are according to translations provided by participants in the seminar. In some cases, the hadiths are excerpts from larger reports. There may be variants with different wording or narrators elsewhere in the Hadith corpus.

1. Ahmad Ibn Hanbal, *Musnad Ahmad ibn Hanbal*, vol. 4, hadith 18596. Translation by members of the Seminar.

2. 'Eisa M. b. 'Eisa Tirmidhi, *English Translation of Jāmi' al-Tirmidhī*, vol. 4. (Riyadh: Dar-us-Salam, 2007), 234. Reprinted by permission of the publisher.

3. Ibn Hanbal, *Musnad*, vol. 6, hadith no. 23879. Translation by members of the Seminar.

4. Muslim Ibn al-Hajjaj, *English Translation of Saḥīḥ Muslim*, vol. 1. (Riyadh: Dar-us-Salam, 2007), 117. Reprinted by permission of the publisher.

5. Al-Suyuti, *Aḥādith* 2, folio 5032:129. Translation by members of the Seminar.

6. Tirmidhi, *English Translation of Jāmi' al-Tirmidhī*, 5:77–78. Reprinted by permission of the publisher.

7. Sayyid Abul A'lā Mawdūdī, *Towards Understanding the Qur'ān*, vol. 3, surahs 7–9 (Leicester: Islamic Foundation, 1990), 202. Rights now held by Kube Publishing (Leicester, UK); reprinted with their permission.

8. Marrakesh Declaration, http://www.marrakeshdeclaration.org/marrakesh-declaration.html. Reprinted with permission of the Forum for Promoting Peace in Muslim Societies (Abu Dhabi, UAE).

9. Abu Dawud, *English Translation of Sunan Abū Dāwūd*, vol. 4, trans. Abu Ammar Yasir Qadhi (Riyadh: Dar-us-Salam, 2008), 388. Reprinted by permission of the publisher.

10. Muhammad b. Isma'il Bukhari, *Ṣaḥīḥ al-Bukhārī: The Translations of the Meanings of Ṣaḥīḥ al-Bukhārī*, vol. 1, trans. M. Muhsin Khan (Riyadh: Dar-us-Salam, 1997), 60–61. Reprinted by permission of the publisher.

11. Dawud, *English Translation of Sunan Abū Dāwūd*, 1:542. Reprinted by permission of the publisher.

12. Muslim Ibn al-Hajjaj, *English Translation of Ṣaḥīḥ Muslim*, vol. 1, trans. Nasiruddin al-Khattab (Riyadh: Dar-us-Salam, 2007), 143–44. Reprinted by permission of the publisher.

13. Tirmidhi, *English Translation of Jāmi' al-Tirmidhī*, 4:253. Reprinted by permission of the publisher

14. Ibn al-Hajjaj, *English Translation of Ṣaḥīḥ Muslim*, 1:150–51. Reprinted by permission of the publisher.

Faith and Political Power

A "Non-Establishment" Reading
of the Christian Tradition

JONATHAN CHAPLIN

In both the Hebrew and Christian scriptures, the people of God—the community of those professing allegiance to God and to God's will for and ways in the world—are depicted as being summoned to stand under, live in conformity with, avail themselves of, and bear public witness to the "power" of God. They are not to scorn or disavow power but to embrace it as God's gift and call. The faithful community is to enact in all the dimensions of its corporate life the vision of a flourishing human condition that God willed for all humanity and that God's redemptive power will, ultimately, realize throughout the whole world.

The people of God thus always had an outward-facing mission. Since biblical Israel was constituted as a religiously unified political community—truly a "nation under God," sharing a common, enforceable religious confession and order of law—the "outward-facing" part of its mission primarily took the form of relations between nations: between Israel and "the nations round about," including members of the latter who happened to be domiciled in Israel ("resident aliens"). The New Testament, however, envisages a radically transformed understanding of how the people of God are to relate to those who are not its members and to the political orders in which the newly constituted people of God can expect to find themselves domiciled. The community of faith now has at its disposal only the "power of the Gospel." This signals an epochal, "dispensational" step-change in God's will for how his people relate to the broader world.

What does this radical change mean for how the people of God are to relate to political orders that do not accept the power of God and may, in some cases, openly repudiate it? To adapt a poignant Hebrew lament, how can the people of God "sing the LORD's song in a foreign land?" (Ps. 137:4). In this chapter I set out what I call a "non-establishment" reading of this fundamental dispensational shift in God's ways of ordering the relation between faith and political power, while acknowledging that there are other readings. My textual focus will be on what came to be regarded in almost all readings as the weightiest Christian text addressing the question, namely, Romans 13. To place this in a larger theological context, however, I open with some broader reflections on "power."

Power as Divine Gift and Call

Mainstream Jewish and Christian traditions have never regarded power as inherently evil. In both traditions it is understood that the community of faith is not given some special, esoteric, "pure" power denied to others but may and must exercise all the kinds of power that humanity itself exercises—all the competencies, capacities, potencies, opportunities, and callings (or vocations) arising from a divinely created human nature and from the divine "plan" for the unfolding of creation in history through human cultural activity: parental power, social power, economic power, intellectual power, artistic power, and so on. To do so is simply to be human, to fulfill the original human task of representing God in the whole of creation—where "representing" means being authorized to bear witness to and extend God's presence and power in creation, thus giving him "glory" (or, to adapt a parallel Islamic phrase, "to make God's cause succeed" in the world). Such power is never arbitrary or capricious but is always given as an enabling resource for humans to realize God's will for the flourishing of all creatures (human and nonhuman). It is power as service to the good of the other—power as one manifestation of love, mirroring the loving, "covenantal" power by which God creates and sustains the whole universe.

The earliest chapters of Genesis suggest that this role of representing God's loving power in creation is at the heart of what it means to be made in the "image" and "likeness" of God (Gen. 1:26). The terms suggest not any ontological continuity between human being and divine being (given the transcendent, majestic "otherness" of God, how could that be?) but rather that humans, uniquely among creatures, are commissioned as God's vice-regents to live in conscious conformity with the divine will in all their dealings with each other and the rest of creation (Gen. 1:26–31).

But that original vocation to exercise God's loving power in all creation has been radically disrupted by "the fall," the rebellious vaunting of self-conferred human power *over against* the loving purposes of the Creator—so that any exercise of human power is now, at best, precarious and fragile, always liable to be corrupted, veering away from divine purposes and so frustrating human flourishing; at worst, it is exploitative, oppressive, idolatrous, even "demonic." Thus, the goal of God's redemptive activity in human history—embracing the entire narrative arc depicted in the Hebrew and Christian scriptures—can be summarized as threefold: to reassert God's rightful power over and in creation, to restore his gracious "rule" or "kingdom"; to overthrow the "power of darkness" (Col. 1:13) and to enact judgment on every human abuse of creation's power, such as by "[bringing] down the powerful from their thrones," as the prophetic Song of Mary has it (Luke 1:52); and to restore humanity's capacity to be (more) faithful stewards of creation's powers—that is, to "renew the image of God" in humanity.

Further, although God's ways are "higher than your ways" (Isa. 55:9), the ways he has called us to exercise power are not inscrutable: God has revealed to humanity—at least, to those "with ears to hear" (Mark 4:9)—how to be faithful stewards of the power entrusted to us: in the perspicuous wisdom of the created order; in the specific revelations in and to Israel ("the word is very near to you" [Deut. 30:14]); in and through Jesus as the fulfillment of Israel (the word made flesh [John 1:14]); and through the subsequent discerning judgments of an authorized community of faith (Matt. 18:18), equipped with the requisite gifts of the Spirit (1 Cor. 12:28). Living in conformity with God's will is thus not a matter of identifying a series of specific injunctions or rules and obeying them to the letter at all times but rather of absorbing and internalizing all the ways in which the divine will is disclosed (i.e., allowing *torah* to be written on your hearts [Heb. 10:16]) and then faithfully discerning and extending their concrete meaning for whatever contexts humans find themselves in—that is, of learning "wisdom."[1]

Political Power

One of many questions arising from this line of thought is whether the powers given originally to all humanity in creation include *political* or *governmental* power. Here postbiblical Christian traditions diverge. Some (Augustine, Martin Luther) hold that such power arises only after "the fall," having been instituted in a special merciful providential act by God to preserve a fallen world from chaos (*fitna*) and violence. Others (Thomas Aquinas and, to some extent, John Calvin) hold that, while the need to exercise corrective, coercive legal power indeed arises only as a result of the fall, the authority to direct and coordinate social life itself arises from the imperatives of created human nature (so that the authority to coerce derives from that prior authority). Both generally assert, however, first, that the power of government (which I shall understand in the normative sense of the "office" of political authority) derives ultimately from God and that humans are, prima facie, obliged to obey it, and, second, that political power is not in the direct gift of the community of faith.

But what, then, is the relation between the Christian community of faith—the church—and the political orders in which it finds itself? In the rest of this chapter I argue, on the basis of Romans 13, that, beyond its own bounds, the church possesses no special power under God than that of peaceful witness to God's loving power.

Reflections on Romans 13:1–7

Long regarded as a charter for unquestioning obedience to any extant government, Romans chapter 13 in fact lays the basis for a critical, conditional theory of
political authority that contrasts sharply with the prevailing Roman imperial
conception. This critical potential has frequently been present in the tradition,
notwithstanding the authoritarian distortions to which it has been subjected by
what was called the theory of "the divine right of kings" (an unhelpful designation,
for few ever doubted that "kings" had a "divine right" of some sort). While there
are certainly specific contextual features that occasion Paul's reflections in this
passage (such as the reference to paying taxes), I suggest that its underlying theology is of much wider significance.[2]

Paul is addressing a church that found itself a marginalized, politically
powerless, and at times a persecuted minority within an oppressive Roman
empire—one that was prepared to tolerate religious minorities so long as they
did not challenge the officially recognized pantheon of pagan deities or question
the authority of the emperor. Paul, as a former Pharisee, would have been fully
steeped in Hebrew texts such as Deuteronomy 17 and Psalm 72—indeed, in the
entirety of the Torah, with its numerous implications for political power. I suggest it is legitimate—indeed, necessary—to read him assuming that kind of for-
mation. Paul would have assumed that all government, not only that formerly
existing in Israel, stood under a divine mandate to promote justice and peace. But
whereas many Jews of the period regarded Roman rule as fundamentally illegit-
imate, albeit necessary to submit to for prudential reasons, Paul reasserts to his
Christian minority readership—some of whom were tempted to think they were
now outside of governmental authority—the same universal mandate of government. Government, he says, generally exists to promote the public good and
punish public wrong. Such rule is legitimate as one of many human "authorities"
appointed by God; Paul says this even though he knew the Roman government
was idolatrous, brutal, and periodically oppressive. Government, he holds, is
appointed, negatively, as the minister of God's vengeance, or "wrath"—it is God's
agent of judgment on injustice, and, positively, promotes good public conduct;[3] for
short, to promote "public justice."[4] Paul seems here to be appealing to the notion
that the very office of government has been divinely established.[5] He does not
take a clear view here on the issue I alluded to earlier, namely, whether political
authority originates in creation or fall. His language seems compatible with
either, but the issue is not, after all, decisive for the question I want to address in
this chapter. But he is clear that the authority of the office of government derives
ultimately from God and that believers (like everyone else) stand under a prima
facie obligation to obey it.

We know from Romans 12 that, within the community of faith, Christians
must renounce avenging themselves. They must not take it on *themselves* to exercise coercive justice when they are subjected to wrong. Rather, they must "leave

room for the wrath of God" (12:19). The injunction not to return evil for evil
does not invalidate the clear mandate of government to secure public justice for
the good of the wider society. Yet this mandate is hedged within robust boundaries. For, as Paul says in Romans 13:4, in fulfilling its mandate, government acts
as "God's *servant* for your good." This is a coded reminder, as Philip Sheldrake
notes in his chapter in this volume, that even the Roman empire is a mere servant,
to whom suitable respect and honor may be due but certainly not worship, and
that it has been appointed not for its own self-aggrandizement but to serve public ends.[6] These normative purposes remain, even if only as a standing indict-
ment of its actual practice. The passage, then, does not teach an authoritarian
theory of political authority but a conditional one: government is theologically
legitimate insofar as it promotes public justice.[7] If it egregiously violates that
mandate, then by implication it loses its legitimacy as a divine servant and
becomes a potentially dangerous, autonomous hegemon of the sort graphically
depicted in the book of Revelation (although what to do in the face of such a
government turns out to be a very complex question in subsequent Christian
practice and commentary).

I submit that Paul's view of the mandate of government for public justice here
is in many ways in keeping with the ancient Jewish theology of the public justice
mandate of government as expressed in passages like Deuteronomy 17 and Psalm
72. But, as indicated earlier, there is one crucial sense in which Paul's political
theology is a profound departure from that ancient theology. If we were to consider only the purely practical point of view, it is obvious that a religious minority
under oppressive pagan rule could not possibly look to government to do what
governments in Israel did, namely, to enforce true religion and eliminate false
ones. Yet this is not merely a prudential accommodation to circumstance, as if
Paul were playing a long game so that when Christians were in a majority they
might seek to restore the confessional polity of ancient Israel. Rather, the refusal
to look to government to define or protect true faith has a fundamental theological grounding, spelled out in Paul's other writings and in the entire New Testament. The task of protecting true religion is now removed from the broader
mandate to promote public justice.[8]

Since Jesus, the very nature of the "community of faith" has changed radically
and irrevocably. God's redemptive purposes are no longer concentrated exclusively in a single territorial community but now embrace every nation. The covenant is now extended to "the Gentiles"—this was the great scandal that proved
so bewildering to the first disciples and to the Jewish communities from which
they emerged. The people of God are no longer a single, unified religiopolitical
community embracing the totality of the life of the community under divine
positive law—and will never be so again: there are no more "covenanted nations."
That dispensation has been superseded forever.[9] The people of God have become
a transnational, nonterritorial, global fellowship of believers united in allegiance
to Christ and in the mission to proclaim the Gospel to all the nations.[10]

The point is not that this mission is now *nonpolitical* but that it is *nonterritorial*, detached from any geographically bounded political community. The kingdom of God is the restored rule of God over every area of human life, and the church must witness to this total reach of God's claimed rule, including its claims on the political order. But such a witness must be pursued by means of a radically different kind of power than coercive legal or political power. Whatever political aspirations it may come to develop when circumstances permit must be pursued without benefit of privileged access to political power, or, rather, with the huge advantage of an entirely different mode of witness to the world—the power of a self-giving love that is willing to suffer for the sake of the Gospel. This mandate for witness is depicted as being delegated directly from the authority of the risen Christ (Matt. 28:18–20). It entails proclaiming and enacting "the Gospel of the Kingdom." It is, exclusively, the authority to testify to the ways in which God is redeeming creation; thus, the apostle Paul speaks of the faithful community as "ambassadors" of reconciliation (2 Cor. 5:20). This *just is* the mission of church in the world: not *itself* to "rule over" those outside the community of faith but rather to witness, in word and deed, to God's ways of ruling, including the ways God intends governments to continue to rule the world (outside the church) within its own allotted sphere of public justice.

This did not mean a posture of passive acquiescence in whatever the empire threw at Christians. As Acts 16:35–40 makes clear, Paul was quite ready to invoke his own rights as a Roman citizen when treated unjustly by Roman authorities—for the sake of the advancement of the Gospel. Nor did it mean that Christians should renounce active participation in political power where circumstances permitted. Among the early Christians were a handful of Roman officials and soldiers, who no doubt would have been catechized in the church to allow their public lives to be informed by the same norms incumbent on the whole church, within the inevitable constraints of a non-Christian society and polity. Most subsequent commentators have held that, since the vocation of government is discharged in a fallen world, it requires the use of legally authorized coercion. When believers found themselves occupying the office of government, they could indeed participate in the exercise of "the sword" just as other any other officeholder did (a point disputed, however, by the sixteenth-century Anabaptists and other later Christian pacifists). Yet, in all the modes of government power, including the coercive mode, believers should seek to steer the use of such power closer to God's original intention for the office of government and, where possible, also toward the future final ("eschatological") renewal of all rule as service-toward-mutual-flourishing. They will, for example, seek from government not *mere* judgment but, as Oliver O'Donovan puts it, "merciful judgement." Christians thus eventually came to regard Matthew 20:25–28 (which can be paraphrased as "you shall not lord it over each other as Gentile rulers do") as applying not only to the internal life of the church but also as informing their exercise of every kind of power, including their participation in government when that became a historical possibility.

Contemporary Implications

Let me briefly sketch seven contemporary implications that I think are consistent with this reading of Romans 13, a passage that I use as a decisive lens through which to discern a coherent, broader ("non-establishment") Christian understanding of faith and political power.

First, contra the "high papalist" view in the Giles of Rome passage, the church must never claim to exercise political authority in its own name. It should seek to act in the political realm as one organization in an open civil society among many others, seeking only the same civil and political rights and freedoms available to any other associations. Members of the community of faith may indeed share in the exercise of political power, alongside others who are not members of that community, just as they may share in any other kind of created power. But they do so not as members of the community of faith (not as bearing the authority of the church) but simply as human beings domiciled in a particular political territory alongside others; that is, as "fellow citizens"—no less, but no more. Sometimes that will require cooperating with what governments already do. At other times it will involve, where circumstances permit, criticizing and correcting it. At still others it could involve opposing governments, even, for some commentators, to the point of resistance (on which a long and complex debate exists in the tradition).

Second, contra Calvin, this excludes the church appealing to government to protect, promote, or privilege its own faith by law or any coercive means. The Calvin passage is but one example of a Christian text in the period of "Christendom" that failed fully to grasp the radical dispensational difference between "Old" and "New" covenants, reverting to the model of the ancient Israelite religiopolitical regime in which government was authorized—indeed, commanded—to enforce the one true religion by coercive law. Tragically, this occurred frequently during Christendom, and wherever it did, especially where it culminated in what Perez Zagorin has termed "the Christian theory of persecution," it amounted to an egregious betrayal of the Gospel, bringing terrible consequences in its train.[11] But the New Testament nowhere even hints that government has or could ever be entitled to exercise such power to enforce true religion.

Third, by implication, government itself must never seek coercively to protect, promote, or privilege *any* faith, including any "secular" faith. This implication points to what much later came to be known as the "religiously impartial" state: not a morally neutral state, as if law did not necessarily rest on certain moral commitments but a state that would acknowledge its inherent religious incompetence and prescind from expressing an official view of the truth or falsity of any ultimate faith or worldview, aspiring to treat all adherents to such ultimate convictions evenhandedly as far as possible in the circumstances. Some Christian theologians term this a "secular" state in the sense of a state that confines itself to matters of temporal, external justice arising in "this age" (the *saeculum*) and leaves matters of "the age to come" (the *eschaton*) to the church.

Fourth, the necessary accompaniment of such a religiously impartial state is the right of all citizens to enjoy maximum individual and corporate religious freedom in private and public spaces, as is affirmed robustly in Vatican II's *Declaration on Religious Liberty.*[12]

Fifth, all this necessarily opens the door for a de facto religious plurality in any state, for as soon as religious coercion is relaxed, it is almost inevitable that divergent faiths will emerge. This does not necessarily imply a positive celebrating or championing of the doctrine of "religious pluralism" either by the state or by others (some Christians claim to find theological reasons for such an affirmation) but only a commitment to the just treatment by the state of a plurality of faiths, within the constraints of public justice.

Sixth, while the above could be termed a "secular" state, it emphatically does not imply a *secularist* state, one that has an explicit intention to impose a secularist worldview on the public realm. Indeed, it opposes it, since full religious freedom and state impartiality will permit religious convictions to play a full part in shaping law and public policy. Government's mandate of public justice includes the securing of protected public space for the articulation of a variety of faiths and worldviews and for the mobilization of support to achieve political objectives flowing from those convictions, within the constraints of law and the constitution. The church has long claimed to have profoundly important things to say on what the faithful discharge of the office of government consists in and will properly seek to equip its members to take up their responsibilities as citizens pursuant to that end. Equally, it is bound to support the granting of the same opportunities for political influence that it seeks for its own member to those of other faiths (religious and secular). For Christians, as for Muslims and others, that will mean exercising all the lawful channels and resources of political power available to them as citizens in order to steer government closer to what they take to be its divine vocation to establish justice in the public realm.

Seventh, and more controversially, the logic of the impartial state militates, in my view, against the church's seeking or enjoying any position of even noncoercive constitutional privilege, such as a religious preamble in a constitution (as in Ireland or Poland), an established church (as in the Church of England), or, by implication, a provision such as that in the Malaysian constitution that "Islam is the religion of the federation." I concede, however, that others hold that the church may in some circumstances properly enjoy a certain spiritual/ceremonial preeminence in public life (the "Establishment" position) so long as this does not in any way compromise the full religious freedom or civil and political equality of others. It is not always clear whether Christian defenders of such provisions would extend them to Islam or other faiths, but it is hard to see how they could decline to do so consistently. Yet, in a situation like Malaysia, conceding the legitimacy of a constitutional provision that privileges Islam over other faiths is having the effect of weakening the power of the publicly marginalized Christian minority to protect its own rights against the successive encroachments of Islamist groups that appeal to such provisions to consolidate their own ambitions for the hegemonic deployment of state power. It is surely preferable to adopt a consistently "non-Establishment" stance, implying state impartiality and maximum religious freedom for all so as to empower embattled and often persecuted religious minorities (of any faith) against any such hegemonic ambitions.

Notes

In this chapter, Bible passages are according to the New Revised Standard Version of the Bible; used by permission; all rights reserved.

1. The content of Torah was not a comprehensive statement of all obligations but an evolving contextual amalgam of commands, statutes, concrete cases, and principles of varying degrees of generality, all framed within the larger narrative of divine salvation, which was to be its interpretive lens. In that necessary process of interpretation, particular commands could change. See Jonathan Burnside, *God, Justice and Society: Aspects of Law and Legality in the Bible* (New York: Oxford University Press, 2012).

2. Here I follow the same exegetical approach as Nicholas Wolterstorff in *The Mighty and the Almighty: An Essay in Political Theology* (Cambridge: Cambridge University Press, 2012), from which I have learned much.

3. The Deuteronomy passage evokes the wider teaching of Torah regarding the twin mandate to pursue righteousness (*şĕdāqâ*, the complex fabric of right relationships marking a human community under God's power) and justice (*mišpāṭ*, the actual delivery of justice, which was to be both speedy and impartial). All Israelites were under this double mandate, yet rulers were under a special charge to do so across the nation as a whole. The just king must act within all the constraints there specified while owning the law of God for himself (he was commanded to write out his own copy, not just leave the law to the Levites who were its primary custodians) and conforming to all its requirements. This is not least so that "his heart be not lifted up above his brethren" (Deut. 17:20 KJV) and so practice injustice against them—the way of "other nations."

4. Oliver O'Donovan uses the parallel term "public judgement" in *The Ways of Judgment* (Grand Rapids, MI: Eerdmans, 2005).

5. Or we might at least say that he is implying that wherever some kind of stable order of government exists that does not systematically tyrannize its people and offers some measure of public justice, it must be construed as legitimate, as a gift of providence for the good of society.

6. In Psalm 72, one of the "royal" psalms portraying an ideally just king, the content of the justice prayed for is entirely in keeping with the detailed depiction of justice throughout Torah, with the special focus here on the king's role of actively securing justice for the poor, the needy, and the oppressed since they are least able to defend themselves. Christians now read this psalm in the light of Christology: the just king is seen as

an anticipation, a prototype, of Jesus Christ, whose kingship effects complete justice and peace for all and whose dominion is universal and everlasting.

7. The John of Salisbury passage is a representative late medieval text containing an extended meditation on what public righteousness and justice entail. Reflecting a variety of biblical and extrabiblical influences, it is composed in the genre of "advice to princes," asserting that law and government office exist to realize an order of divine justice ("equity") and are wholly subordinate to that purpose. It is profoundly informed by biblical passages such as Deuteronomy 17 and Psalm 72; indeed, it expounds the Deuteronomy passage at some length, describing the prince as "the minister of public utility and the servant of equity," especially charged with shielding the weak and innocent from the depredations of the strong.

8. This view, admittedly, was rejected in mainstream political theology for much of the 1,500 years of what we know as "Christendom." See, e.g., Oliver O'Donovan and Joan Lockwood O'Donovan, eds., *From Irenaeus to Grotius: A Sourcebook in Christian Political Thought* (Grand Rapids, MI: Eerdmans, 1999).

9. This is not, however, to suggest that from a Christian theological point of view the Jewish people have now disappeared from divine history, that their status as "chosen" people has been abolished—a deeply problematic view known as "supersessionism." Paul himself seems clearly to reject such a view in Romans 11.

10. This community does have its own *internal* sphere of power: the authority of that special, redemptive institution called "the church," as addressed in Joan O'Donovan's chapter in this volume.

11. Perez Zagorin, *How the Idea of Toleration Came to the West* (Princeton, NJ: Princeton University Press, 2003).

12. See Carolyn Evans, "The Second Vatican Council on Religious Freedom," in *Justice and Rights: Christian and Muslim Perspectives*, ed. Michael Ipgrave (Washington, DC: Georgetown University Press, 2009), 129–45.

Christian Texts for Dialogue on Faith and Political Power

Deuteronomy 17:14–20

[14]When you come to the land which the Lord your God gives you, and you possess it and dwell in it, and then say, "I will set a king over me, like all the nations that are round about me"; [15]you may indeed set as king over you him whom the Lord your God will choose. One from among your brethren you shall set as king over you; you may not put a foreigner over you, who is not your brother. [16]Only he must not multiply horses for himself, or cause the people to return to Egypt in order to multiply horses, since the Lord has said to you, "You shall never return that way again." [17]And he shall not multiply wives for himself, lest his heart turn away; nor shall he greatly multiply for himself silver and gold. [18]And when he sits on the throne of his kingdom, he shall write for himself in a book a copy of this law, from that which is in charge of the Levitical priests; [19]and it shall be with him, and he shall read in it all the days of his life, that he may learn to fear the Lord his God, by keeping all the words of this law and these statutes, and doing them; [20]that his heart may not be lifted up above his brethren, and that he may not turn aside from the commandment, either to the right hand or to the left; so that he may continue long in his kingdom, he and his children, in Israel.

Psalm 72:1–10, 15b–19

[1]Give the king thy justice, O God,
    and thy righteousness to the royal son!
[2]May he judge thy people with righteousness,
    and thy poor with justice!
[3]Let the mountains bear prosperity for the people,
    and the hills, in righteousness!

⁴May he defend the cause of the poor of the people,
  give deliverance to the needy, and crush the oppressor!
⁵May he live while the sun endures, and as long as the moon,
  throughout all generations!
⁶May he be like rain that falls on the mown grass,
  like showers that water the earth!
⁷In his days may righteousness flourish,
  and peace abound, till the moon be no more!
⁸May he have dominion from sea to sea,
  and from the River to the ends of the earth!
⁹May his foes bow down before him,
  and his enemies lick the dust!
¹⁰May the kings of Tarshish and of the isles render him tribute,
  may the kings of Sheba and Seba bring gifts!
  . . .
¹⁵ᵇMay prayer be made for him continually,
  and blessings invoked for him all the day!
¹⁶May there be abundance of grain in the land; on the tops of the mountains
  may it wave;
    may its fruit be like Lebanon;
    and may men blossom forth from the cities like the grass of the field!
¹⁷May his name endure for ever, his fame continue as long as the sun!
  May men bless themselves by him, all nations call him blessed!
¹⁸Blessed be the Lord, the God of Israel,
  who alone does wondrous things.
¹⁹Blessed be his glorious name for ever;
  may his glory fill the whole earth!
  Amen and Amen!

Romans 13:1–7

¹Let every person be subject to the governing authorities. For there is no authority except from God, and those that exist have been instituted by God. ²Therefore he who resists the authorities resists what God has appointed, and those who resist will incur judgment. ³For rulers are not a terror to good conduct, but to bad. Would you have no fear of him who is in authority? Then do what is good, and you will receive his approval, ⁴for he is God's servant for your good. But if you do wrong, be afraid, for he does not bear the sword in vain; he is the servant of God to execute his wrath on the wrongdoer. ⁵Therefore one must be subject, not only to avoid God's wrath but also for the sake of conscience. ⁶For the same reason you also pay taxes, for the authorities are ministers of God, attending to this very thing. ⁷Pay all of them their dues, taxes to whom taxes are

due, revenue to whom revenue is due, respect to whom respect is due, honor to whom honor is due.

Acts 16:35–40

[35]But when it was day, the magistrates sent the police, saying, "Let those men go." [36]And the jailer reported the words to Paul, saying, "The magistrates have sent to let you go; now therefore come out and go in peace." [37]But Paul said to them, "They have beaten us publicly, uncondemned, men who are Roman citizens, and have thrown us into prison; and do they now cast us out secretly? No! let them come themselves and take us out." [38]The police reported these words to the magistrates, and they were afraid when they heard that they were Roman citizens; [39]so they came and apologized to them. And they took them out and asked them to leave the city. [40]So they went out of the prison, and visited Lydia; and when they had seen the brethren, they exhorted them and departed.

John of Salisbury, *Policraticus:* Book 4[1]

Chapter 2. [The law and the prince]: Princes should not suppose that they are disparaged by the belief that the justice of God, whose justice is eternal justice and whose law is equity, is preferable to the justice of their own statutes. Furthermore, equity (as the experts in law assert) is a matter of what is appropriate, according to which reason equalises the whole and seeks equality in matters of inequality; what is equitable to all is what grants to each person that which is his own. Its interpreter is law, inasmuch as law makes known the will of equity and justice. . . . All are, for this reason, obligated to be restrained by the necessity of observing the laws, unless perhaps someone imagines that he is granted the licence of iniquity.

Still the prince is said to be an absolutely binding law unto himself, not because he is licensed to be iniquitous, but only because he should be someone who does not fear the penalties of law but someone who loves justice, cherishes equity, procures the utility of the republic, and in all matters prefers the advantage of others to his private will. But who in public affairs may even speak of the will of the prince, since in such matters he is not permitted his own will unless it is prompted by law or equity, or brings about judgments for the common utility? For in fact his will in these matters should have the force of judgment; and that which most rightfully pleases him in all matters has the force of law because his determination may not be inconsistent with the design of equity. "From your visage," it is said, "My judgment proceeds, your eyes must look at equity" (Psalms 17:2), for indeed the uncorrupted judge is one whose determination is on the basis of the assiduous contemplation of the image of equity. The prince is therefore the minister of the public utility and the servant of equity, and in him the public persona is borne since he punishes all injuries and wrongs, and also all crimes, with moderate equity. . . . While his shield is also strong, still it is a shield for the feeble and one which deflects the darts of malignance from the innocent.

Chapter 6. [The ruler and God's law]: "When he sits upon the throne of his kingdom, he will write for himself a copy of this law of Deuteronomy in a book." See that the prince must not be ignorant of law and, although he takes pleasure in many privileges, he is not permitted to be ignorant of the laws of God on the pretext of the martial spirit. The law of Deuteronomy, that is, the second law, is therefore to be written in the book of his heart so that the first law, which is impressed upon the page, corresponds to the second, which is recognised by the mystical intellect. The first could be written on stone tablets; but the second was not imprinted, except upon the purer intelligence of mind. And the prince properly writes Deuteronomy in a book because he may thus reflect upon the law in his reason without the letter disappearing from before his eyes. And hence, the letter of the law is followed in such a fashion that there is no divergence from the purity of its spirit. For in fact the letter destroys, while the spirit confers life, and with the ruler rests the moderate interpretation of human law and equity in accordance with necessity and general circumstance.

John Calvin, *Institutes of the Christian Religion* (1559) Book 4, Chapter 20[2]

The duty of magistrates, its nature, as described by the word of God, and the things in which it consists, I will here indicate in passing. That it extends to both tables of the law, did Scripture not teach, we might learn from profane writers; for no man has discoursed of the duty of magistrates, the enacting of laws, and the common weal, without beginning with religion and divine worship. Thus all have confessed that no polity can be successfully established unless piety be its first care, and that those laws are absurd which disregard the rights of God, and consult only for men. Seeing then that among philosophers religion holds the first place and that the same thing has always been observed with the universal consent of nations, Christian princes and magistrates may be ashamed of their heartlessness if they make it not their care. We have already shown that this office is specially assigned them by God, and indeed it is right that they exert themselves in asserting and defending the honour of him whose vicegerents they are, and by whose favour they rule. Hence in Scripture holy kings are especially praised for restoring the worship of God when corrupted or overthrown, or for taking care that religion flourished under them in purity and safety. On the other hand, the sacred history sets down anarchy among the vices, when it states that there was no king in Israel, and, therefore, every one did as he pleased (Judges 21:25). This rebukes the folly of those who would neglect the care of divine things and devote themselves merely to the administration of justice among men; as if God had appointed rulers in his own name to decide the earthly controversies, and omitted what was of far greater moment, his own pure worship as prescribed by his law.

Pope Paul VI, *Dignitatis humanae* (Declaration on Religious Freedom)[3]

Subtitle: On the right of the person and of communities to social and civil freedom in matters religious, promulgated by His Holiness Pope Paul VI on December 7, 1965.

2. The Vatican council declares that the human person has a right to religious freedom. Freedom of this kind means that everyone should be immune from coercion by individuals, social groups and every human power so that, within due limits, no men or women are forced to act against their convictions nor are any persons to be restrained from acting in accordance with their convictions in religious matters in private or in public, alone or in association with others. . . .

It is in accordance with their dignity that all human beings, because they are persons, that is, beings endowed with reason and free will and therefore bearing personal responsibility, are both impelled by their nature and bound by a moral obligation to seek the truth, especially religious truth. They are also bound to adhere to the truth once they come to know it and to direct their whole lives in accordance with the demands of truth. But human beings cannot satisfy this obligation in a way that is in keeping with their own nature unless they enjoy both psychological freedom and immunity from external coercion. Therefore, the right to religious freedom is based not on subjective attitude but on the very nature of the individual person. For this reason, the right to such immunity continues to exist even in those who do not live up to their obligation of seeking the truth and adhering to it. The exercise of this right cannot be interfered with as long as the just requirements of public order are observed.

3 . . . . All are bound to follow their conscience faithfully in every sphere of activity so that they may come to God, who is their last end. Therefore, the individual must not be forced to act against conscience nor be prevented from acting according to conscience, especially in religious matters. The reason is because the practice of religion of its very nature consists primarily of those voluntary and free internal acts by which human beings direct themselves to God. Acts of this kind cannot be commanded or forbidden by any merely human authority. But the social nature of the human person requires that individuals give external expression to these internal acts of religion, that they communicate with others on religious matters, and profess religion in community. . . .

11. God calls people to serve him in spirit and in truth. Consequently, they are bound to him in conscience, but not coerced. God has regard for the dignity of the human person which he himself created; human persons are to be guided by their own judgment and to enjoy freedom. This fact received its fullest manifestation in Christ Jesus in whom God perfectly revealed himself and his ways. For Christ, who is our master and Lord and at the same time is meek and humble of heart. . . .

He did not wish to be a political Messiah who would dominate by force but preferred to call himself the Son of Man who came to serve, and "to give his life as a ransom for many" (Mk 10:45). . . . He recognized civil authority and its rights when he ordered tribute to be paid to Caesar, but he gave dear warning that the greater rights of God must be respected: "Render therefore to Caesar the things that are Caesar's, and to God, the things that are God's" (Mt 22:21). Finally, he brought his revelation to perfection when he accomplished on the cross the work of redemption by which he achieved salvation and true freedom for the human race. For he bore witness to the truth but refused to use force to impose it on those who spoke out against it. His kingdom does not establish its claims by force, but is established by bearing witness to and hearing the truth and it grows by the love with which Christ, lifted up on the cross, draws people to himself.

Taught by Christ's word and example the apostles followed the same path. From the very beginnings of the church, the disciples of Christ strove to persuade people to confess Christ as Lord, not however, by applying coercion or with the use of techniques unworthy of the Gospel but, above all, by the power of the word of God.

Notes

In this chapter, all Bible passages are according to the Revised Standard Version (RSV).

1. John of Salisbury, *Policraticus: Of the Frivolities of Courtiers and the Footprints of Philosophers*, trans. Cary J. Nederman (New York: Cambridge University Press, 1990), 30–31, 41. Reprinted by permission of the publisher.

2. John Calvin, *Institutes of the Christian Religion*, trans. Henry Beveridge (Edinburgh, 1845), 1174.

3. Austin Flannery OP, gen. ed. Laurence Ryan, trans. *Dignitatis Humanae (Declaration on Religious Liberty): A Completely Revised Translation in Inclusive Language* (Collegeville, MN: Liturgical Press, 2014), 552–53, 554, 560, 561–62. Originally published by Dominican Publications, Dublin, Ireland, 1996. Excerpts from documents of the Second Vatican Council are from *Dignitatis Humanae: Declaration on Religious Liberty*, ed. Austin Flannery, OP, © 2014. Used with permission of Liturgical Press, Collegeville, Minnesota.

PART FIVE

Reflections

Conversations on Power

Some Reflections on Building Bridges Seminar 2017

LUCINDA MOSHER

"To be honest," recalls Azza Karam,

> as a new invitee into this dialogue and coming into it from a so-called poli-cymaking international secular institution (the United Nations) as a non-theologian, my time at the Building Bridges Seminar left me with a feeling akin to what it must have been like for Alice in Wonderland—minus any evil figures. Every encounter (reading of texts; conversation) was a discov-ery. Some challenged what I thought I knew—about my own faith (Islam) and what I understand to be the 'Christian' faith. And indeed, it occurred to me that some of the challenges were, in themselves, affirmations.

The degree of learning that characterizes every convening of the Building Bridges Seminar, which has met annually since 2002, is made possible, as Karam puts it, by features of this initiative "which the organizers have clearly honed, over time": the regularity of annual meetings; the degree of selectivity applied to choosing the participants; the careful thought put into assigning the readings from the Bible, Qur'an, and other sources—and to the juxtaposition thereof.

To Karam's mind, however, the most interesting ingredient—and most partic-ipants over the years would echo her sentiment—is the Seminar's commitment to and method of small-group discussion: "its formula of constructing 'study groups' whose members remain constant as they keep convening and discussing, in a very well-moderated manner, over the course of several days; the manner in which questions for pondering and studying are posed; and the subsequent daily reconvening of the whole group for sharing and further reflection." When reporting on these conversations, it has long been the practice of the Seminar to observe the Chatham House rule: participant comments and questions are recorded without attribution. Nevertheless, participants are often eager to share what they themselves have taken away from these discussions. Thus the written reflections of four individuals who were, in 2017, newcomers to Building Bridges Seminar and whose thoughts on that meeting were solicited some six months after it adjourned. Ovamir Anjum is the Imam Khattab Chair of Islamic Studies at the Department of Philosophy, University of Toledo (USA). Jonathan Chaplin, an independent scholar who formerly served as director of the Kirby Laing Institute for Christian Ethics (2006–2017), is currently a member of the Divinity Faculty of Cambridge University (UK) and a senior fellow of the Canadian Christian think tank Cardus. Azza Karam is senior advisor at the United Nations Population Fund and coordinator of the United Nations Inter-Agency Task Force on Religion and Development. Elizabeth Phillips, a Christian theologian, is currently a Visiting Scholar in the Institute for Criminology at the University of Cambridge (UK). The reflections of these four—two women, two men; two Muslim, two Christian—inform this summary of the nature and content of the Seminar's deliberations on power "at a moment when so many attendees, like so many people in the rest of the world, were feeling distinctly powerless."

The Building Bridges Seminar Style

"As a first-time participant in the Building Bridges Seminar I could not have known precisely what to expect from our small-group sessions," says Elizabeth Phillips; "but what I realized I had not expected was how very little most of us knew of the other faith." Her small group comprised scholars who, like her, had colleagues who study both Christianity and Islam, or who had been involved in various kinds of interfaith dialogues and initiatives—as had she.

> One would reasonably expect that we would each have at least elementary working knowledge of each other's traditions, but this was only really true of one member of our small group—someone who is a practitioner of one faith and scholar of the other and so had effortlessly fluent knowledge of both. The rest of us were asking very basic questions of one another. Although we were discussing high-level matters concerning divine and human authority and power, along the way we were learning rather entry-level aspects of the content and contours of each other's texts and traditions. I sometimes felt surprised at the minimal knowledge of certain aspects of Christianity which was revealed by the questions of Muslim scholars in the group—then would quickly realize the hubris which was revealed by my feeling of surprise. For what possible reason should I expect any Muslim scholar's understanding of Christianity or the Bible to be more substantive than my own very limited understanding of Islam and the Qur'an? These revelations were both indictment and opportunity. On the one hand, it was an indictment of our inattention to one another in our everyday lives and

work. And if we who are scholars of theology, religious studies, and other disciplines related to our faiths, many of whom work in universities along-side scholars of other faiths, know so little of one another's convictions and practices, what might this indicate about the majority of the people who practice our faiths?

"I came as a specialist in Christian political thought but a beginner in Islam," Jonathan Chaplin explains:

> It was not the first Muslim-Christian encounter I had participated in but it was the first intensive that was focused on texts, and in the presence of scholars from both faiths. It was a transformative experience. It reaffirmed emphatically that, in seeking to understand the sacred writings (and the existential dynamics) of another faith there is simply no substitute for being in the physical presence, over an extended period of time, of persons com-mitted to, immersed in, and struggling to make contemporary sense of, those texts. For me it was an immense privilege to meet, learn from and converse with Islamic scholars of great learning, integrity, and generosity, who also shared a common striving not only for fidelity within the commu-nity of faith but also for justice in the wider world. Although I'd read *about* the Qur'an before, I came away with the sense that, for the first time, it was no longer a forbidding, "alien" text but one I could now begin to read with some orientation, discrimination and appreciation. It was also poignant to see that my experience was mirrored among my fellow Muslim partici-pants, whose genuine curiosity about and, in some cases, positive enthusi-asm for, passages in the Christian Bible was clearly evident.

Ovamir Anjum calls the Building Bridges Seminar 2017 "one of the most pro-ductive intellectual engagements with colleagues I have ever had."

> At the communal level, such meetings are entirely unpredictable and their intellectual content always a reflection of the uneven education of the par-ticipants, the power differential between different participants, insufficient knowledge of the basic scriptural and communal issues at hand, and the desire to be pleasant and acceptable, all of which often lead to little edifi-cation and long-term development. I still strongly advocate such dialogues, but they should be rethought as intercommunity dialogues, in which the goal formally ought to be what is often realized ex post facto: communal goodwill and friendships that transcend religion or theology. Dialogues that build bridges of understanding at a lasting level, however, require trust, time, and prior training. At Building Bridges, I was persuaded that actual interfaith dialogue at the highest level is possible and highly desir-able for academic and intellectual development of Islam and Christian faith

traditions, precisely because of the carefully studied conditions maintained by the stewards and organizers of the program as well as its continuity which allows continual tinkering and improvement. It will not be going too far to suggest, therefore, that Building Bridges is establishing a new tradition of dialogue that has the promise to affect Christian and Islamic scholarly traditions, bringing them in closer dialogue, in a significant and lasting manner. Neutrality of conviction is neither possible nor desirable, nor will any dialogue ever take place without differentials of power and resources and without immediate concerns, but what is attainable is genuine concern to learn and engage, to teach and persuade, engage in giving and receiving criticism, and appreciate each other's humanity and scholarship at work, not to mention building lasting friendships. This genuine concern is what I found most valuable and moving at the Seminar, carefully cultivated by the leadership.

As a native Arabic-speaker whose childhood learning of the Qur'an has been expanded by independent study with Sunni and Shi'a clerics at different times, and who now works "in fields which are removed from theology," Azza Karam admits she often finds her "understanding of the meaning of scripture is not necessarily in sync" with scholars of Islam per se. Thus, she says, "I thoroughly enjoyed having the opportunity to learn from and pose questions to the Islamic scholars participating in the Seminar alongside me."

During the 2017 discussions, Karam recalls, there were times when she felt more of a commonality of understanding with some of the Christians—especially with the women—than with the Muslims in her group—"even to the point of having the same questions about the text and the meaning." This was particularly the case, she says, "when we were seeking to understand themes like the absolute sovereignty of God, or the call to 'fight the disbelievers.'" At other times, she stresses, "I marveled at the fact that some of the Christian colleagues appeared perturbed by references in the Qur'an related to the 'wrath of God,' and yet there seemed to be echoes of just that in some of the biblical references. So why, I wondered aloud, is one reference to God's wrath less 'understandable' than another?"

Karam's mention of her freedom and willingness to "wonder aloud" calls to mind that, indeed, at the core of the Building Bridges style is its provision of the "opportunity to ask honest questions unashamedly," as Elizabeth Phillips describes it. In fact, she continues:

The ease with which we were quickly able to ask such questions opened up important conversations which allowed us to begin to grasp the basics, through and alongside our topics of discussion which were complex. One such conversation in our group arose during our discussions of whether/how communities of faith can/should exercise power. Within these complex and thorny questions, we also pursued a conversation about the significance of the Meccan and Medinan eras, and the surahs of the Qur'an arising from them. Some believe it is important to distinguish the Meccan from the Medinan: in the earlier, Meccan period Muhammad functions as prophet and in these surahs he teaches nonviolence and mercy; in the later, Medinan period Muhammad functions as statesman, and in these surahs he sets out laws and introduces jihad. These different eras and surahs are read as exemplifying contrasting perspectives on, experiences of, and relationships to authority, power, and violence.

Some would say there are significant analogies between the Mecca/ Medina contrast and questions which arise for Christians concerning the contrast between Hebrew narratives of conquest, monarchy, and nationhood, and New Testament teachings on enemy love, nonviolence, and martyrdom. While there are important and significant differences (e.g., both the Meccan and Medinan periods are of the Prophet, and the two are encompassed within his lifespan, while Hebrew and Christian scriptures are before and after the Christ event, and they span centuries), there are also significantly similar attendant questions (e.g., are the Meccan/New Testament teachings more "universal," while the Medinan/Hebrew narratives were more particular to a time and place?). Perhaps unsurprisingly, just as many Christian scholars would reject a dichotomized view of old-versus-new as reductionistic, some Muslim scholars insist on more holistic readings of the Qur'an. While knowledge of these issues and perspectives is undoubtedly of the most elementary order, the quality of encountering the conversation through discussions with and between Muslim scholars of different schools of thought on the subject was also an exceptionally rich introduction.

Such dialogical reading of scripture is at the very heart of the Building Bridges Seminar's method—an aspect of the experience that many participants have extolled. "Only when looking at the texts so carefully, side by side, and in the presence of scholars of all the three scriptures, could one note both the enduring similarities and differences," Ovamir Anjum notes. "Both are quite instructive. The similarities between the Qur'an and the Old Testament, on the one hand, and the Qur'an and the New Testament, on the other—each better understood and appreciated in conversation with the other two—have been my food for thought since the 2017 Seminar concluded."

Some Topics of Conversation

God's Role in History

For Ovamir Anjum, the very practice of dialogical intertextual study brought to the fore a thematic difference between the scriptures of Christianity and Islam regarding the notion of God's role in history. He explains:

It has been often noted that the Abrahamic traditions emphasize linear history rather than nature as the fundamental cosmic narrative, and I have been dutifully teaching my students the same. Our Building Bridges conversations made me realize an added layer of complexity. Unlike the Bible, the Qur'anic story telling is remarkably cyclical. A remark by a Christian kicked off the conversation which then planted the idea of a seminal contrast in my mind, namely, that God in the Qur'an appears to be the creator and master of nature, the Great Designer, whereas in the Old Testament, we sense God's nature unfold in history. God, in the Qur'an, appears far to be above history; God of both history and nature. Whereas in the Bible God's intervention in human affairs, unpredictable and hence conducive to an unfolding, uncharted history, the Qur'anic story is predictable, subject to timeless laws, to what the Qur'an calls the sunan (customs) of God.

"You do get glimpses of the inner life of God in the Bible," said the Old Testament scholar in my group, "but they are not abstracted." The biblical tradition, she noted, "is focused on what God is doing rather than what He is in Himself." Furthermore, another scholar stressed that the Bible "is polyphonic; there are numerous voices present." The Qur'an, he noted, "witnesses to a constant pattern or cycle with the prophets." This made me think of, first, the similarity. The Qur'an too speaks of God's "discovering" through the unfolding of human history: "We found that most of them did not honor their commitments; We found that most of them were defiant" [7:102], says the Qur'an after relating several stories of prophets, their followers, and their detractors. However, such language in the Qur'an is rare and ambiguous; the overwhelming message of the Qur'an being that it is God's eternal attributes that are important, that give rise to certain patterns in history, and that are expressed in what Muslim tradition came to call the Ninety-Nine Names of God. God in the Qur'an always saves His people in the same kind of way, unfailingly, based on the adequacy and faithfulness of the humans involved. Nothing humans do seems to take God by surprise or alter His custom. In the Bible, in contrast, while God's general omnipotence might be unquestionable, His intervention in human affairs appears unpredictable.

Another element that adds to the biblical sense of historicity in comparison to the Qur'an's unicity of theme and mood is obviously their different modes of compilation, but what I came to appreciate is how the fact that at times commentary on scripture itself becomes scripture for later generations preserves a wonderfully complex sense of interaction within the text. The Qur'an clearly conceives of itself as continuing and commenting on the earlier scriptures, but it does not reproduce those scriptures at length; it sees itself as correcting or confirming rather than commenting on the earlier scriptures.

Prophethood

Relatedly, says Ovamir Anjum, intertextual consideration of divine and human power led fruitfully to insight into the contrast between the biblical and Qur'anic presentation of prophets. "This pertains," he notes,

> to the humanity and complexity of biblical prophets, who err and have conflicting human drives, versus the single-minded devotion of the Qur'anic prophets, whose errors are acts of negligence quickly set right by God's vigilance and overwhelming forgiveness. Whereas the Qur'anic prophets are not quite as perfect as the later Muslim tradition presents them, they stand in marked contrast to the biblical presentation of prophets as at times tragically flawed figures. Earlier Muslim scholars were extensively aware of and employed biblical materials for exegetical purposes, as is well-known, but I do think that a renewed emphasis on a dialogical reading of the Qur'an with faithful yet rigorous biblical scholarship promises to be productive and rejuvenating for the Islamic exegetical and theological tradition, far more so than the many secular revisionist currents, which have been ignored or found unworthy of engagement by the Muslim high tradition.

Faith and Justice

Of the many things that struck Jonathan Chaplin "with particular force" was how Muslims see the relationship between faith and justice:

> The sense of a common commitment to the struggle for justice in the wider world—as one of the many ways in which humans are to respond to, and seek to see realized, "God's power"—was clear throughout. No one felt the need to argue the point because all present shared the view that such a commitment was integral to their faith tradition, however differently it might be worked out. That shared commitment, by the way, is something I do not always experience when conversing with fellow Christians, at least with those who focus inordinately upon the inner personal life of faith at the cost of a full recognition of and participation in God's larger purposes of justice in the world. Certainly, some instances of real disagreement surfaced between Christians and Muslims as to what justice actually requires: for example, how far does it require or permit full individual religious freedom, in a society shaped overwhelmingly by a dominant faith, by those of a different faith or of no faith. But then such disagreements have always existed, of course, also among Christians, as they do among Muslims. Yet the experience of a common commitment to a justice-oriented faith left me with a sense of deeper bond with Muslims than I had experienced before.

The Necessity of True Faith

Chaplin reports that, for him, deliberations during the seminar brought renewed clarity to another dimension of the faith-justice relationship: the notion of the necessity of "true faith." He explains:

> Those Muslims who have interpreted their own tradition as favoring or mandating an official recognition of Islam, at least in Muslim-majority states, and perhaps as mandating unequal standing for non-Muslims in such states, are, I now see more clearly, motivated by the fundamental conviction that *without true faith there can be no human justice.* I think I now grasp more fully that, at its best, this conviction is not driven by a desire that the true faith (still less its human advocates) dominate for its own sake, nor that true faith can in fact be coerced (both traditions have central texts that deny this explicitly), but that, without true faith—unless the true God is worshipped rightly—human society is plunged into a state of extreme fragility, rendered deeply vulnerable to disorder and arbitrary violence. This is evident in several of the Qur'anic texts we read, as it is, of course, in many others. What was particularly fascinating here was the reminder that the Christian tradition itself harbors a parallel conviction about "true" faith and "true" justice. It was Augustine (claimed by every strand of the Christian tradition) who famously, and momentously, wrote that, "true justice is found only in that commonwealth whose founder and ruler is Christ" (*City of God*, book 2, chapter 21). The Christian tradition has, however, read that assertion in profoundly divergent ways. Some have read it to require that, given the lack of access to true justice by unbelievers, believers (namely, the church) must exercise power over political authorities—*for the sake of human justice.* Thus, Giles of Rome, in a passage we read, claims that "earthly power . . . will have no capacity to judge what is just or unjust except insofar as it does this by virtue of (a delegated) spiritual power." Others have read Augustine's assertion to mean that, since true justice is only present where there is true worship, believers must come to terms with living in substantially unjust societies (in "this age," the *saeculum*), albeit ones in which they are called to be faithful witnesses to true justice within the possibilities historically (i.e., "providentially") afforded to them. There are, of course, several mediating positions between the two.
>
> Since, in the paper I presented to the Seminar, I argued for a version of the second reading, I found it salutary to be confronted with the fact that, in Islam, the former reading has by far been the most dominant historically and is not some minor or eccentric reading. But while I continue to struggle with the very idea of an official political privileging of any faith, I came away conscious that I must more fully reckon with the fact that those who

would defend Islamic political "privilege"—who might, for example, hold that, ultimately "Islam must rule"—at best do so out of a radical commitment to the better realization of human justice in the present, something to which my faith also commits me. That, of course, is what also motivates those in my own tradition who might lend support to, for instance, a modest constitutional or symbolic privileging of Christianity (while yet defending full religious freedom for others). So I have some work to do here. Let me simply suggest, however, that if we were to focus our conversations on normative political order on the question of "how better to secure human justice" rather than on "whose faith is true" or "whose faith should rule" (while not suspending those questions), we will likely discover significant areas of agreement on what proximate political goals to work for (greater economic, ecological, and gender justice, for instance) in those many contexts where neither of our faiths fully "rule" or are ever likely to. And since in both traditions perfect justice is seen as unattainable prior to final divine judgment, we face the common challenge anyway of how our societies might be edged incrementally toward greater justice.

God's Vulnerability

"A well-known observation of participants in interfaith (as well as intrafaith, ecumenical) conversation," Elizabeth Phillips reminds us, "is that when we carefully attend to encounters between differing traditions, we each learn about or reflect in new ways upon our own traditions at least as much as we learn about other traditions." She describes, as a personal example, the opportunity afforded her during the seminar to reflect on Hosea 11:8–9 and to consider this biblical passage "in light of both the expertise offered by the Hebrew scripture specialist in the group and the questions offered by Christians and Muslims alike." She explains:

> This verse came at the end of a passage we considered under the heading of "God's Power and Vulnerability in Conflict." Written in the divine first person, the passage laments that although Israel/Ephraim was treated with the tender care and provision of a parent for a child, they had turned away and forsaken YHWH. But the divine response is not wrath: "My heart recoils within me; my compassion grows warm and tender. I will not execute my fierce anger; I will not again destroy Ephraim; for I am God and no mortal, the Holy One in your midst, and I will not come in wrath."
>
> Our conversation focused in on the word "for," and its implication that *because of* the divine nature there would be tenderness and mercy. The force of the passage is not that *even though* YHWH is divine and could execute righteous wrath, an act of condescension would result in mercy. Rather, *because* YHWH is divine—is YHWH—Israel is spared and protected.

Later the same day we revisited the same theme in our discussion of the Christ Hymn in Philippians 2. Verse 6 of this hymn is often translated with an *although* at the beginning: "Although he was in the form of God . . ." However, there is no *although* in the original and it has been widely observed that it might also be translated "Because he was in the form of God . . ." That is, Jesus's humble self-emptying was not *in spite of* his divine nature but *because* of it.

Our group went on to consider the obedience of verse 8 in this regard: that Jesus "became obedient to the point of death." While some theories of atonement would understand this as the obedience of the son to the father, we discussed it in terms of Jesus's obedience to his own divine nature, resonating with our reading of Hosea 11:8–9. In addition to the significance of this discussion in terms of theology and Christology, this connection between the portrayal of divine nature in the Hosea passage and the divine nature of Christ in the Philippians passage also served to illustrate the point that dichotomized readings of the two testaments of Christian scripture are unsustainable.

Indeed, the thought that God could be "vulnerable" was a lively topic in Jonathan Chaplin's group as well. He explains:

In his stimulating opening lecture, Jonathan Brown claimed that Islam could be construed as a "corrective to the Jewish and Christian notions of God's vulnerability."[1] This is because, from an Islamic point of view, God's power is absolute and limitless, admitting of no "bargaining" (as in the paradigmatic case of Abraham's pleading on behalf of Sodom) such as one witnesses in Jewish and Christian notions of divine "covenants" with humans. In our further conversations it became clearer to me that in Islam, while, on the one hand, God appoints humans as his "vice-regents" (thereby establishing them as radically equal to one another), that God's dealings are invariably "just," that God is willing to show "infinite mercy" in his dealing with wayward humans (mercy being one of the divine names), and that the Qur'an itself "invites" humans into a "dialogue" (as a member of our group put it) so that they may recognize its truth; on the other, Islam lacks a sense of God "taking risks" in his dealings with creatures—that he could be so deeply implicated with humans, bound in a relationship of such intimacy, that he might be rendered "vulnerable" by those dealings.

Once again, there are parallels to this apparent tension in the Christian tradition. There is, for example, a longstanding debate in systematic theology about God's "impassibility" (the claim that God cannot experience pain or suffering, or indeed anything like a human emotion). The question shows up narratively in Scripture in, for example, God's apparent "wrestling" with his own declarations, on the one hand, that he is "sovereign ruler of heaven and earth," and, on the other, the "covenantal longings" toward faithless human beings that lead him to exclaim, "but I cannot give you up."

While there are evident differences within each tradition on the question, the starkness of the gulf between them on the basic matter at stake has left me with the intriguing and disturbing question of what difference this makes to matters of political order and justice. How, in other words, will our search for human justice be affected by whether we worship a vulnerable or an invulnerable God?

The Theological/Political Intersection

For Azza Karam, it was both a challenge and an affirmation to realize that, as a nontheologian (albeit a practicing believer), she had learned a great deal from the *thawy al-'ilm* (Those Who Know; i.e., the Learned Ones [theologically]) who were her colleagues in the seminar.

But I realized I was learning because I was allowed to think aloud, in a safe space, by sharing some of the geopolitical realities which were not necessarily part of the theological realm. I refer specifically to two distinct aspects which fed into the discussions around power, but which are distinctly nontheological, or marginally so. One of these aspects concerns some of the discourse of political Islam, or Islamism, for instance, being able to reflect on the fact that the understanding of vengeance in Luther's essay *On Temporal Authority*[2] was very similar to Sayyid Qutb's logic in *Milestones*[3]—Qutb often being seen as the original "architect" of Islamist thinking. Another aspect relates to the positions and dynamics related to working with some governments and with faith-based organizations—i.e., different realities which feed into and are resulting from geopolitical discourses, such as when sharing and discussing the Marrakesh Declaration.[4] In other words, I was learning because I was able to bring in different experiences relating to another aspect of how the two faiths intersect with more worldly matters.

The Seminar's Uniqueness

Few come to a convening of the Building Bridges Seminar as novices to dialogue. Ovamir Anjum's prior experience had included many years of work as a fellow at the Lubar Institute for the Study of Abrahamic Religions at the University of Wisconsin–Madison, and engagement at community-level interfaith meetings since well before such efforts mushroomed in the wake of the attacks of 9/11/2001. Years of work at the United Nations had afforded Azza Karam numerous dialogical engagements. "I could not help but compare my experience of

Building Bridges," she says, "to another attempt which I had been part of, many years back, which regularly convened social scientists and policy makers around Middle Eastern politics. The objectives were very similar. But the Middle Eastern politics discussion deliberately eschewed theology or theological conversation—assuming these would only be divisive; and it had grown to well over 200 participants." What rendered Building Bridges a special learning experience? At the least, three main things, Karam asserts:

> Firstly, size matters, and knowing when a number is "sufficient" to be conducive to an informative dialogue that does not grow unwieldy, is a skill—and a blessing. Secondly, consistency matters. Here I refer to the fact that the same people met in the same study group over a relatively long period of time. (Five days is not a two-day meeting experience.) And yet, learning from the well of the wider participants was still possible when the whole of the group was also regularly (but not exhaustingly) reconvened. Thirdly, how we listen to one another matters, and it helps a great deal when there is a shared culture of civility of discourse.

Over the course of several well-structured days together, many complex questions and concepts were fruitfully discussed and explored. This is characteristic of the Building Bridges Seminar. "Yet," says Elizabeth Phillips, "I wonder if the other members of my group, like me, also left with unasked and unanswered questions. Perhaps the most significant unspoken question for me did not concern the texts we were reading about power, but our own power and limitations of power as participants in this seminar." She explains:

> On the one hand, as a group we possessed a rather stunning degree of power: accomplished scholars with platforms for giving voice to the importance of interfaith encounter, employed by institutions which give us the luxury of participating in such initiatives as this, backed by very large sums of money generously given to make our travel and very comfortable accommodation possible. On the other hand, I could not help feeling something of a sense of powerlessness: what could we actually do, collectively and/or individually, with and after this experience which might effect any level of transformation in the communities and faiths we represented? How could we most positively, responsibly, and responsively exercise the evident power we held as a group and as individuals? It felt a bit like being given a lavish gift, opening it with great delight and gratitude, then not being entirely sure what was meant to be done with it now opened.
> This sense could, of course, point toward a critique which some have leveled against these sorts of "elite" interfaith gatherings and conversations because, on this view, the most significant and transformative encounters must be grassroots and/or activist rather than academic. I am an ethicist

and political theologian with an activist personality, so these critiques resonate with me to a significant degree. However, what they seem to assume is that interfaith encounter is somehow zero-sum: Are we going to invest in elite, intellectual encounter? Or grassroots, practice-based encounter? Or activist, transformative encounter? The reality is that there is no reason to accept this zero-sum premise. Each of our traditions requires for its health, longevity, and faithfulness a complex economy of scholars and theologians who devote themselves to intellectual exploration of the faith, groundedness in the devotion and practice of the faithful grass roots, and new horizons pursued by pioneers and activists who speak truth to power and work for transformation of structures and societies. For what reason should we trust the assumption that interfaith encounter is legitimate in only one of these registers? It seems clear to me that the hope of building significant bridges between our two faiths requires work in all these modes.

I do not intend to brush aside too easily questions about the power and privilege represented in our gatherings. But the question of what is to be done with this lavish gift, now that we have opened it, need not be one of frustration that this particular gift does not serve the same purpose which other gifts will and do serve. It may in fact be a question of patience. What is to be done with the gifts of grassroots and activist encounters may seem more immediate and readily apparent; what is to be done with the ways in which each of our intellects, theological frameworks, and scholarly pursuits have been transformed by this encounter may unfold more slowly, seeping into our lives and work and the lives of those around us in numerous ways, noteworthy and unnoticed, but transformative nonetheless.

Certainly, this particular gathering together of Christian and Muslim scholars and texts, with sufficient time for high-quality interaction with both, had allowed for a range of perspectives within the two traditions to be in conversation interestingly and fruitfully. Why exactly does the Building Bridges Seminar work? Azza Karam says that, in all honesty, she is not sure. "I am not sure if UK- and US-based theologians (as most participants were) are relatively better disciplined when it comes to listening, and listening well, and differing respectfully. Or whether the Building Bridges architects are very wise and fortunate in their selection of participants. Or both. Or perhaps there may indeed be truth behind the adage that wonderful things happen when people come together to speak of, and with, the Divine—because God joins them."

Notes

1. See Jonathan Brown, "The Power of God and Islam's Regime of Power on Earth," earlier in this volume.

2. Martin Luther, *Temporal Authority: To What Extent It Should Be Obeyed*, trans. J. J. Schindel, rev. by W. I. Brandt, *Luther's Works* 45 (Philadelphia: Fortress, 1962).

3. *Maʿālim fī'l-Tarīq* (1964), published in English as *Milestones*, is a treatise by Egyptian Islamist Sayyid Qutb putting forth a plan for the revival of Islam.

4. *The Marrakesh Declaration on the Rights of Religious Minorities in Predominantly Muslim Majority Communities* was the outcome of a summit, January 25–27, 2016, organized by His Majesty King Mohammed VI in conjunction with the Forum for Promoting Peace in Muslim Societies. The executive summary is included in the present volume. See p. 131f.

Subject Index

Note: A separate index follows for Scriptural Citations.

egalitarianism, 13, 14; hierarchy of power outside of, 15; non-Muslims not equal to Muslims, 15

Egypt: Hezekiah's desire for alliance with, 54; Moses's confrontation with Pharaoh and exodus from, 26, 39, 54, 55–56, 96; Pharaoh's arrogance, 55; sun worship and deities in, 21–22

Enoch, First Book of, 37–71, 58

equality: among Christian gifts and services, 104; among Muslims, 80; constitutional privilege of state religion and, 146–47, 164–65; of minorities in Muslim societies, 121

eschatology, 38, 58, 71, 99, 101–2, 105–6, 111, 144

ethics: maxims based on, 123, 136; virtue ethics, 120

Ethiopian Bible, 1 Enoch 37–71, 58

evil: Christian believers' awareness of, in order to resist, 99; consequences of evil deeds made to seem fair, 39, 48; God's inability to do, 12; Holocaust and, 17n11; modern Christian theologians on, 17n11; overcoming with good, 104, 112; power not inherently evil, 140; premodern Christians' view of, 17n11; Qur'anic commandment to resist, 82

existential or moral worth, 14

exodus from Egypt, 21–22, 26, 54, 96; Red Sea, God's parting of, 55–56, 68–69

exorcism, 22, 58

expulsion as punishment, 102, 105

the fall, 140, 141

forgiveness, 2, 22–23, 32, 46, 130; among community of believers, 80, 90, 99–100, 104, 110; baptism and, 111; God's forgiveness of all sins, 47; Jesus instructing Peter to forgive his brother's sins against him, 102, 110; in Lord's Prayer ("Our Father"), 100, 110; texts advocating, in contradiction to other texts, 122

Forum for Promoting Peace in Muslim Societies, 121, 132

free choice, 37, 38, 93, 132

freedom of religion. See religious freedom

French church, fight between Boniface VIII and Philip IV for jurisdiction over, 106

French Orientalists, 10

friend-friend relationship, 14. See also community of believers, fellowship as conceived in the New Testament

Fromentin, Eugène, 16n5

gender differences, 14

Gentiles, 72, 103, 104, 139, 143

Giles of Rome: On Ecclesiastical Power, 106, 113–14, 145, 164

godliness, commitment to, 79, 82

God's power: chaos defeated by, 51–56; compared to Pharaoh's and Egyptian gods' power, 21–22, 55–56; in cosmogony, Exodus, and liberation from exile, 53–54, 66–67; deference to, 12; difficulty in delineation of, 31–32; divine action, decree, and intervention, 36–39, 46–49, 162; as Divine Warrior, 51–53, 56, 65; as infinite power, 21–22, 31–32, 166; in Jesus Christ's life and actions, 22–23; as liberating power, 26; majesty as apt way to characterize, 32; metaphors and parables of in Qur'an, 10–11; moral ordering of natural world and, 16; no negotiation possible with, 11, 166; omnipotence of, 21–22, 24, 31, 33, 37, 38, 39, 48, 66, 162; omniscience of, 34, 37, 39; portrayal of, 9–10; predeterminism and, 37, 39, 49; of protection, 12, 34; questions on, 2; Qur'an as expression of and testament to, 32; Rahman on, 32; suffering servanthood revealing, 56–57; as "superlative of all superlatives" in Qur'an, 10, 12, 44; theodicy and, 11–12; trust in, 12; vulnerability in conflict and, 57, 165–67; YHWH, 51–53, 165. See also creation; forgiveness; God's wrath; mercy

God's role in history, 39, 49, 161–62

God's wrath, 38, 47, 59, 105, 111, 142, 143, 150, 160, 165

Good Samaritan, 25–26

grass-roots interfaith dialogue, need for, 168–69

Great Commission, 20

Gutiérrez, Gustavo, liberation theology of, 19, 26

Hadith, 11; Abu Da'ud, 135; Ahmad ibn Hanbal, 127; al-Bukhari, 38, 47, 88, 135; Muslim, 39, 49, 81, 88, 91, 127, 135, 136; Al-Muttaqi al-Hindi, 88; al-Suyuti, 127–28; al-Tirmidhi, 89, 91, 127, 129, 135–36

healings by Jesus, 22–23, 58, 71

Hellenic tradition, 9

heretics, protecting God's power from, 12

Herod Antipas and Herodians, 24

Hezekiah (king), 54–55

Vatican II's *Declaration on Religious Liberty*, 146
vicegerency or stewardship role, 36, 46, 78, 87–88, 140, 141, 166
virtue ethics, 120
vulnerability: consideration for, 102; of God, 57, 70, 165–67; human society's condition of, 164; impassibility of God and, 166; purposeful and powerful, 59; sheep's courage when confronting natural foe of wolf, 56–57

warfare. *See* armed conflict
Watt, William Montgomery, 122
wilaya (friendship), 78
wisdom, 1, 23, 72–73, 141

Wolterstorff, Nicholas, 147n2
women: as Building Bridges Seminar participants, 1, 158; commonality of understanding by, 160; in Muslim community, 78, 88; in relationship to power of men, 14–15; religious freedom of, 153; seizing of, in discord between factions, 79
worship acts, 95
wrath of God. *See* God's wrath

Yam, 58

Zagorin, Perez, 145
Al-Zamakhshari, 84n11
Zion theology, 54–55
Zulus, 15

Scriptural Citation Index

About the Editors

Dr. Lucinda Allen Mosher, assistant academic director of the Building Bridges Seminar, is faculty associate in interfaith studies at Hartford Seminary and an affiliate of its Macdonald Center for the Study of Islam and Christian-Muslim Relations. Concurrently, she is the Center for Anglican Communion Studies Fellow in World Anglicanism at Virginia Theological Seminary and president of NeighborFaith Consultancy LLC. Mosher is the author or editor of a number of books and essays on multifaith matters. She received her ThD from General Theological Seminary (New York City).

The Rev. Dr. David Marshall is academic director of the Building Bridges Seminar—an initiative he helped to launch in 2002, while serving as chaplain to the Archbishop of Canterbury. Presently, he is the programme executive in interreligious dialogue and cooperation at the World Council of Churches in Geneva, with particular responsibility for Christian-Jewish and Christian-Muslim relations; and a research fellow at Georgetown University's Berkley Center for Religion, Peace, and World Affairs. He studied theology at Oxford University and holds a PhD in Islamic Studies from the University of Birmingham.

CPSIA information can be obtained
at www.ICGtesting.com
Printed in the USA
BVHW082155111119
563547BV00002B/4/P